Girls Uncovered is a heart-wrenching, eye-opening exploration of the current sexual realities among young women in America. Doctors, counselors, pastors, and parents all ought to read this book in order to gain better understanding of the challenges young women face today in the fight for true physical and emotional health that leads to a bright future. It is an enormously valuable resource for those of us responsible for the teaching and protecting of our young women.

    —JOSH MCDOWELL, author and speaker

Girls Uncovered paints a compelling and sobering portrait of the sexualization of young women in today's society. In this book, McIlhaney and Bush tell us how premarital sex puts young women at risk—emotionally, socially, and physically—and what parents and professionals can do to help steer young women clear of the shoals of America's contemporary sexual culture.

    —BRADFORD WILCOX, Director of the National Marriage
       Project at the University of Virginia

JOE S. MCILHANEY JR., M.D. AND FREDA MCKISSIC BUSH, M.D.

WITH STAN GUTHRIE

GIRLS UNCOVERED

NEW RESEARCH
ON WHAT AMERICA'S
SEXUAL CULTURE
DOES TO
YOUNG WOMEN

NORTHFIELD PUBLISHING

CHICAGO

Edited by Annette LaPlaca
Interior design: Rose DeBoer
Cover design: Faceout Studio

Library of Congress Cataloging-in-Publication Data

McIlhaney, Joe S.
  Girls uncovered : new research on what America's sexual culture does to young women / Joe S. McIlhaney, Freda M. Bush ; with Stan Guthrie.
     p. cm.
  Includes bibliographical references and index.
  ISBN 978-0-8024-6298-5
  1. Teenagers—Sexual behavior—United States. 2. Teenagers—United States—Attitudes. 3. Adolescent psychology—United States. 4. Sex (Psychology) I. Bush, Freda McKissic. II. Guthrie, Stan. III. Title.
HQ27.M35 2011
306.70835—dc23

                                                          2011035657

All websites and phone numbers listed herein are accurate at the time of publication, but may change in the future or cease to exist. The listing of website references and resources does not imply publisher endorsement of the site's entire contents. Groups and organizations are listed for informational purposes, and listing does not imply publisher endorsement of their activities.

We hope you enjoy this book from Northfield Publishing. Our goal is to provide high-quality, thought-provoking books and products that connect truth to your real needs and challenges. For more information on other books and products written and produced from a biblical perspective, go to www.moodypublishers.com or write to:

Northfield Publishing
820 N. LaSalle Boulevard
Chicago, IL 60610

1 3 5 7 9 10 8 6 4 2

Printed in the United States of America

For J. Thomas Fitch, M.D.,

highly respected San Antonio pediatrician since 1968,

past president of the Texas Pediatric Society,

committed chairman of the The Medical Institute board of directors

from 2001 to 2011,

and a constant source of encouragement and enthusiasm

to all who know and work with him

Contents

CHAPTER ONE

Hopes, Dreams, and Fears

FROM THE MOMENT their daughter is born, moms and dads sense the unmistakable call to protect and guide her toward a fulfilling life. Their optimism for this beautiful child almost always shows on their faces—but so, too, does the weight of the task ahead. And the challenges in our increasingly sexualized culture are many, and, in some ways, multiplying. That's why we have written this book, *Girls Uncovered: New Research on What America's Sexual Culture Does to Young Women*. We want to guide parents so they in turn can guide their girls safely through the challenges they will face to achieve their potential and enjoy full health, hope, and happiness.

The guidance we're offering is born out of our own lives, both professionally and personally. We are obstetricians who have delivered hundreds of baby girls. But we have also taken care of these girls as they grew into young women and we have dealt firsthand with the sexual issues they have confronted.

We both have raised or are raising daughters, so we have, like other parents, had to apply what we know with those we love. These are not simple issues for either of us, and we will not be offering the usual bromides and pat answers. We will instead provide you with solid, research-based information in an easily digestible format so that you can help your daughter safely navigate today's sexual culture.

As doctors and parents with years of experience and research, we've concluded that the standards of today's sexual culture—namely, that

> *We sound the alarm, not to limit young women's sexual lives and futures, but to enhance them—indeed, to rescue them.*

young women engage in sex with many partners, starting at a relatively young age—simply aren't in young women's best interests. The new sexual norms for young people don't lead to the outcomes that young women consistently say they want, as measured by virtually any indicator of health and well-being. We want to sound the alarm, not in order to limit young women's sexual lives and futures, but in order to enhance them—indeed, to rescue them.

Sometimes it seems as if your daughter doesn't want to be rescued—but she does. Most parents wonder at times whether their children are bothering to listen to them at all. It takes a lot of patience, skill, and forgiveness to communicate with an adolescent. Is all the effort worth it? When you're faithfully attempting to pass on your hard-won wisdom, your child may respond with an infuriating look that says, "I know all this, I don't like your telling me this now, and I don't ever want to hear it again."

Your effort is worth it, but communicating with your daughter is hard work. It takes time. And it will come as no surprise that none of us has enough time these days, and we all have a thousand excuses why we can't take the time to hang out with our children or why a meaningful conversation can wait until tomorrow. We've all been there. It is reassuring to know our failure to be at one important recital or ball game will not send our daughters down the wrong road. But the fact is, if we don't purposefully, intentionally spend time with a daughter now, if we don't build into her a commitment to connect into our family life, the fulfilled woman we desire to see in a few short years may never emerge.

And just on a practical level, time spent with your daughter now may help you avoid even greater expenditures of time and money later—on unhappy items such as family counseling, drug or alcohol rehab, health problems, and so on. An old commercial for automobile air filters featured a repair man saying, "You can pay me now, or pay me later." When it comes to safeguarding the well-being of our daughters, it's much wiser to pay a little bit now rather than a lot later.

But of course time and money are the least important reasons to connect with our daughters. We want to see our precious daughters flourish. Most Americans can agree at least on the basics of what that flourishing looks like. Pollster Frank Luntz points out that 54 percent of Americans say that having a loving family is highly important. Also highly important to us are good health (50 percent), financial security (43 percent), and happiness (33 percent).[1] All this doesn't just happen. We must help build into our daughters the habits that can facilitate this good future.

So you want your daughter to be a grounded person and to discover "who she is," not who pop culture tells her she should be. Trends or peers often offer only a shallow or even counterfeit picture of reality and what type of person she should become. A girl who grows up without sound guidance is vulnerable to making poor decisions and setting unworthy goals.

You, however, can have a dramatic impact on your daughter's future—really. Scientific surveys clearly reveal that more girls say their parents influence their behavior than girls say peers, media, or any other sources are influencing their lives. This parental guidance is vital if we want a child to grow into a successful and fulfilled person. By the way, talking the talk is not nearly enough; we must also walk the walk. Our actions must match our words. Young people seem to have a sixth sense for detecting hypocrisy. It is almost no use urging our daughters to live healthy lives if we are not willing to pursue healthy habits ourselves.

A major study of college women highlights this fact. Norval Glenn and Elizabeth Marquardt, in *Hooking Up, Hanging Out, and Hoping for Mr. Right: College Women on Dating and Mating Today*, interview women from intact families and report: "Several women reported that they learned about guys and relationships not so much by talking with their parents, but by observing them. One woman said her ideas come 'probably mostly from my parents and seeing the way my dad treats my mom.'"[2]

Parents with children who are about to become teenagers know that it is a scary time. They hear of teenagers in other families involved in drugs, binge drinking, and promiscuity. They hear of unplanned pregnancies. They hear of unhappy girls who are wasting their time, led astray by peers. They rightly worry about all these things.

In our offices, both of us have seen the unhappy result of these behavior choices hundreds of times. Joe treated a twenty-one-year-old woman who had been engaging in sex since she was fourteen. She had had eight to ten "partners" by this time and was coming in with a severe gynecologic problem that was a result of her sexual encounters. Through the years many other young women with similar stories followed this young woman through his office with difficult problems needing treatment from multiple sexual contacts. Freda saw a fourteen-year-old girl who had been sexually active since age twelve with a total of fourteen boys. But the girl said this behavior was okay because, "I only have sex with my boyfriend."

But we want to encourage you. This is a book of hope. Many parents do not fully understand the sexual culture their daughters face today and how they can help these young women to navigate it well. There are things you can do *now* to minimize the chances of your daughter making poor choices ahead. You can increase the odds that your child will achieve her potential. What are those things?

The research is very clear. Studies of people who have grown up to be healthy, caring, and responsible adults—the kind of people you want your daughter to become—reveal some fairly specific behaviors their parents engaged in that contributed to the good outcome in their lives.

> Simple things can have an enormous impact for good on our children.

The Search Institute, which has been studying such people for years, has developed a list of forty "building blocks of healthy development" that it calls "Developmental Assets." First on the list for every age group is the ability of the family to exhibit high levels of consistent love and support for the children.[3]

Just what such support might look like is laid out in the largest longitudinal study ever done on adolescents—the "National Longitudinal Study of Adolescent Health," or just Add Health.[4] Add Health reports that children are more likely to be healthy, happy, and engaged in good behavior (avoiding risky behavior) if their parents are physically present with them at specific times: when they get up, when they come home from school, when they eat dinner, and when they go to bed.[5] This is not rocket science, but it is challenging to "be there" for our children, given the many things that tug at our time and energy.

Researcher Luntz confirms the findings of the Search Institute and the Add Health study. He offers some parental behaviors that can help children develop well. First on his list is having dinner together.[6] Again, simple things can have an enormous impact for good on our children. We will delve into them much more extensively in a later chapter.

While helping your daughter can sometimes seem tiring, you probably have an unexpected ally: your daughter. Despite all the stereotypes about teen rebellion, teens *are* listening.[7] Young people who enjoy a good connection with their parents and communicate well with them are not only less likely to be involved in sex but are less likely to be involved in alcohol and drug abuse, violence, and so on.[8] So even when your daughter gives you a dumb, stupid, or blank look, just keep talking. You are probably influencing her behavior more than either you or she may realize.

This is *good* news. Parents' desires for their children and their important role in helping those dreams become reality dovetail perfectly with what young women tell researchers they desire for their own lives. These desires of young women include their academic goals, their career goals, their family life goals, and their overall aspirations for life.

Occasionally desires like these are addressed in large, nationwide surveys, as a way of monitoring the development of youth across the United States. One such study, called "Monitoring the Future,"[9] surveys high school seniors about their educational, career, and life aspirations, yielding some interesting insights.

Many high school girls are ambitious. They expect to have a professional career. About one in four say they want a job that requires a doctoral degree, while another 40 percent say that they want to have a professional career, such as nursing or engineering, that does not require a doctoral-level degree. More girls than boys want to have a career as a professional. Only 1.6 percent of girls say they aspire to be a full-time homemaker, though of course there is nothing wrong with this choice. And most girls do not see their careers as temporary, only filling the time until they are married and have children. Some 95 percent of girls say it is quite important or extremely important for them to be successful in their chosen field.

More than 80 percent of teen girls say they would continue to work in their chosen field even if they had enough money to live comfortably. Fewer boys report they would do the same. These results show how driven American girls are about having careers—especially ones that demand large quantities of time and education.

And how do these young women plan to prepare themselves for those jobs? It turns out that these girls take their academic success very seriously. More girls than boys claim they consistently try to do their very best work in school. These girls have high goals for their education and career and are actively laying the groundwork to achieve them.

What about their goals for marriage and family? High school senior girls, it turns out, feel as strongly about succeeding in that part of their life as in their careers. More than 90 percent say that it is important for them to have a good marriage and family life. Only about 5 percent say that they do not want to be married at all. And more than 80 percent say it is likely they will stay married to the same person for life.

What about kids? Most (70 percent) agree that being a mother and raising children is "one of the most fulfilling experiences a woman can have." Only a very small minority of surveyed girls (around 6 percent) say it is unlikely that they will have children. The most popular answer these girls give for the number of children they want is two, but more than 40 percent want *three or more* children.

Do these success-oriented goals for career and family decline as girls become young women and enter college? You might suspect so, but the evidence shows otherwise. Academic and career goals remain very important. For the 2007–2008 school year, many more women than men were enrolled in graduate school. Women received more master's degrees and a similar number of doctoral degrees. Additionally, women account for a greater proportion of the increases seen every year in enrollment into graduate schools.[10] In the early 1980s, only about a third of medical school graduates were women. In 2009, about half were.[11]

What about teen girls' aspirations for family life? One national survey of 1,000 young women in colleges across the US reveals that they retain the family goals they held in high school.[12] More than four out of five say that marriage is an important goal. Almost every young woman (96 percent) agrees that if she does get married, she wants her marriage to last a lifetime. And most (86 percent) *expect* that their marriage will endure. Another large national study asked women aged twenty to twenty-four how many children they expect.[13] Almost half expect to have two children, while almost a quarter foresee having three. Very few say they will have no children at all.

So teen girls and young women have very ambitious plans through high school and college. They expect to perform well in school and to establish themselves in a stable career, all without sacrificing marriage and family life. Thus, parents' desires for their daughters and daughters' desires for themselves are very similar.

But what is happening to those dreams? Are girls attaining the goals they have set for themselves? In many cases, the answer is no. The US Department of Education reports that about 6 percent of girls drop out of high school. When the girls are asked why they did so, 28 percent cite pregnancy and 25 percent cite motherhood.[14] When you look at the eighteen- to twenty-four-year-old girls who successfully completed high school, fewer than 50 percent are enrolled in college.[15] Of those who do enroll in a four-year program, about 17 percent drop out within two to three years. "Personal reasons," cited by more than 60 percent of these girls, is by far the most common answer given for dropping out of college.[16]

A breast-feeding consultant told Freda that she saw a postpartum mother who was fifteen years old. The teen mother said that she wanted to become an obstetrician-gynecologist. The consultant noted later that this teen didn't seem to have a clue about how much more challenging she had made it for herself to achieve that dream by having a baby at age fifteen.

Why do the dreams of so many young women get crushed? It's true that sometimes dreams die because of unavoidable life events, such as a devastating auto accident. Sometimes unrealistic expectations do the job, such as a person with clumsy hands wanting to be a neurosurgeon. Far too often, however, these dreams fail to come to fruition because of choices that could have been made differently. This is what makes us so sad—and is one of the primary reasons for this book.

One dramatic example of a young woman's dangerous choices comes from the book *Hooking Up, Hanging Out, and Hoping for Mr. Right*. A young woman says, "'I think hooking up with different people and seeing what you like and don't like is a good idea. Because eventually you're going to have to . . . marry someone and I'd just like to know that I experienced everything.' Although it is admirable to take risks and learn from one's mistakes, these women would probably find it difficult to explain how having your heart broken a few or even many times in your early years—or trying to separate sex from feeling, as in hooking up—is good preparation for a trusting and happy marriage later on."[17]

> *Your role in helping your daughter reach her goals is critical.*

And of course early hookups and breakups are *not* good preparation. The divorce rate is frighteningly high. Data we will show later point out that people who have had multiple sexual partners and who cohabit before marriage are more likely to divorce if they do marry. Many unmarried teen and college women are therefore engaging in sexual behavior that may be harming one of their key desires—a lasting marriage.

Your role in helping your daughter avoid such problems and reach her goals is critical. These desires and goals are exciting. They don't just happen, but for girls even to have these thoughts at least gets them started on the right track. Though raising a girl is complicated and sometimes heart-rending, be encouraged. A few core activities you can build into your family life will increase the likelihood that your girl will enter adulthood with a strong foundation that can lead to a truly happy life.

And that strong foundation will reach deep, well below the surface. We're not just talking about developing the positive behaviors that will enable her to reach the goals that you both desire—as good as those behaviors may be. We're talking about inner strength, resolve, and commitment. Interestingly, scientists tell us that your daughter's brain is being molded during these important years, for good or ill. Involved parents are actually positively influencing the physical development of their daughter's brains. Such healthy brain molding will help your daughter to acquire healthy habits for life. While we will discuss this much more later, we simply want to point out that you can do a lot more for your daughter than simply provide her with a veneer of good behavior. What you do can go deep. It can change the very structure of her brain as she grows.

So when that little girl was placed in your arms, you were given a great responsibility. You looked into the eyes of a new and beautiful person with her own unique design and potential. For many of us, however, our joy at such times is mingled with fear. How will this vulnerable person turn out, and how can I protect her?

The gift of a daughter is an exceptional opportunity. In many ways this little one is a blank slate for you to write on. What you write will affect her for the rest of her life. If you write poorly, your daughter may be an incredibly happy and successful person anyway. However, if you write well, you remarkably improve her chances for and may pave the way for her to more easily achieve the happiness, health, and fulfillment both she and you desire. Let's get started on writing well.

CHAPTER TWO

Girls: Covered or Uncovered?

WESTERN SOCIETY HAS what a fair-minded observer might conclude is a schizophrenic attitude toward girls. On the one hand, we celebrate their potential and take them to our workplaces to encourage their aspirations. To help them reach their potential, we fiercely protect them against anything that could hurt them or knock them off course. We are on the alert against sexism, bullying, and many other dangers.

Yet on the other hand, we display a curious lack of concern about a certain vital area in their lives. We are failing to guide them in male-female relations, romance, love, sex, commitment, marriage, and so on. The contrast is startling and poses real dangers for the daughters we love.

Throughout history, most societies have carefully protected their young women from potentially harmful sexual involvement. Parents, reinforced by most social institutions, would give their daughters reasons to avoid sex until they settled down, generally, with one man. In the past, women lived in community, learning how to feed and care for their infants, often in otherwise very hostile environments. These arrangements protected them from sexual predators, among other dangers. Essentially, societies agreed on these guidelines and restrictions for the good not only of the individual but, more importantly, of the entire community. Maintaining this hedge of protection has been one of society's most important roles for millennia, for from the reproductive capacity of their girls will come future generations. For some isolated groups, protecting their women has been literally a matter of life or death.

In *Hooking Up, Hanging Out, and Hoping for Mr. Right,* Glenn and Marquardt point out that past societies have

recognized sets of rules and expectations that helped women think about what they wanted when it came to love, sex, commitment, and marriage. In an earlier time the pathway to marriage had a name, "courtship," a word that now seems as quaint as the practices it described. The University of Chicago scholar Amy Kass writes that in our present situation "there are no socially prescribed forms of conduct that help guide young men and women in the direction of matrimony. . . . Even—indeed especially—the elite, those who in previous generations would have defined the conventions in these matters, lack a cultural script whose denouement is marriage." Although it is clear that our campuses lack a culture of courtship, Kass makes clear, and we agree, that we do not want to "roll back the clock," nor would we want to abandon women's gains in social status and power. "If courtship or something like it is to come back," she concludes, "it must do so under vastly different social conditions, and it must no doubt adopt different forms."

Yet, the question might still be asked, why does our postmodern, egalitarian society need to occupy itself with a nineteenth-century sounding notion like courtship? One reason is that having access to social scripts and clear norms helps people to deal with the inevitable ups and downs of romantic love. Another reason is that, particularly regarding sexuality and romance, social norms not only constrain individual self-expression, they also facilitate and empower it. Without such norms, people struggle to create order all on their own and, typically, when they cannot achieve this tall order, they blame themselves when things go wrong.[1]

While considering the question of whether adults should concern themselves with the romantic relationships of youth, the authors continue:

One of the historical features of courtship was that parents and other older adults were actively involved in overseeing and guiding the social lives of their daughters and the young men who expressed interest in them. Throughout history the mating of young adults has rarely if ever occurred in a vacuum, but instead has taken place in a thick nexus of social relations that included older adults who helped to influence young people toward good marital choices. Yet today, it appears that older adults, including college administrators and social leaders who have access to the young through education, media,

Young people need our active and constant help.

health professions, and more, seem largely to have withdrawn from this role.[2]

Despite their native intelligence and all the advantages we can give them, all babies, young children, and adolescents are vulnerable. They are vulnerable to being hurt. They are vulnerable to being influenced for good, and they are vulnerable to being influenced for bad. There is a reason they have been given parents.

A huge part of the reason for their vulnerability is simply physiological. In chapter 6, we will discuss how our brains are not fully mature until our mid-twenties.[3] This fact has huge implications. The portion of the brain slowest to develop and last to mature is the part that enables us to foresee the consequences of our actions. It is the part that guides moral judgment. It is called the prefrontal cortex. Using MRIs and other sophisticated tools, neuroscientists can demonstrate the immaturity of the prefrontal cortex until well into our twenties.

That's why children constantly need cues from the people around them and from the larger society about how to act, what to do, what is important, what is right, and so on. They simply are not yet fully equipped to embrace what are known as the four cardinal virtues—*courage, temperance, justice,* and *wisdom.* Young people need our active and constant help. We will discuss the full implications of this astounding truth later. But it is clear that the long-standing desire of earlier societies to protect young women had a far firmer foundation than we might have expected.

> *We give them no reasons to limit their inborn sexual desire, a desire that is healthy and good but demands certain limits.*

American society, however, has torn down this hedge of protection. In doing so, we have left our adolescents and young women naked, uncovered, and unprotected. We give them no argument that would enable them to say no to the sexual desires of young men. Further, we give them no reasons to delay and limit their own inborn sexual desire, a desire that is healthy and good but demands certain limits. In abandoning our protective role for young women, we have abandoned one of our most vital social obligations.

A child's brain, indeed an adult's brain, in some ways is like a giant computer. We have all heard the phrase "garbage in, garbage out." When garbage thoughts and ideas go into our heads, garbage will come out later in harmful behavior and destructive decisions, which can also hurt everyone around us. When a young girl is left without healthy guidance about her sexual behavior, it is almost certain that she will act on the garbage her mind has been receiving from our sexualized culture.

While we might automatically think of television and film as the main conduits of this culture, it has now spread to, and in turn is spread by, cyberspace and the digital world. Computers and the Internet, cell phone calling and texting, MP3 players, Facebook, MySpace, Twitter, and other digital tools produce a river of words, music, pictures, and ideas that flood a young person's brain. According to a recent study, teenage girls send an average of 4,050 texts a month, while teen boys send an average of 2,539.[4]

And these are not just *any* texts! One out of every five teens reports sending a nude or partially nude photo of himself or herself by cell phone or e-mail. These pictures usually go to friends, but 15 percent of teens say that they have sent nude or seminude pictures to someone they knew only online.[5] Of course, this also means that approximately this percentage has received nude or suggestive e-mail pictures.

This is only the start of the threats from these technologies. MP3 players can pipe songs with very destructive words and themes directly into your daughter's brain. We would print some of those lyrics here, but they verge on the pornographic. Why don't you try listening to your daughter's iPod and find out for yourself? The experience could be sadly enlightening.

Pornography is easily available via the Internet, too. In fact, it can pop up even when a curious teen is not searching for it. The ongoing scandal of adults posing as teenagers and preying on young teens has been well documented. One in seven children ages ten to seventeen who uses the Internet has been sexually solicited online.[6]

We emphasize these threats to young women not to curse the technologies themselves, which can be exciting and useful tools for young people. But keep in mind that a tool is only as useful as the purpose to which it is put. An ax can be used to kill another person, but it can also be used to chop down a dead tree. The ax is not bad in itself. It all depends on how you use it. We believe these technologies, though potentially dangerous, can be made useful if their risks are controlled. (We will discuss ideas for accomplishing this in chapter 9.)

Movies, DVDs, video games, and television shows should all carry a large sign: "Warning, could be hazardous to teen health." Sexual jokes, activity, innuendos, and nudity are rampant in media today. One reliable study of adolescents and television shows that 70 percent of programs popular with teens had sexual content, and 8 percent contained explicit or implicit intercourse. On average, each hour of programming popular with teens has 6.7 scenes with sexual topics.[7]

Studies show almost as much sexual content in music videos as in television programming. Sexual intimacy is shown in from 60 percent to 75 percent of these videos. The visual imagery is often much more sexualized than the music and words.[8]

A thorough study of teens and media titled "Impact of the Media on Adolescent Sexual Attitudes and Behaviors" shows that the media popular with young people—including television, music videos, music, movies, magazines, advertising, video and computer games, and the Internet—are often permeated with sexual content.[9]

Young people are immersed in all kinds of media. One reliable study shows that American children aged eight to eighteen spend an average of 7.5 hours per day with some form of media, an increase of more than an hour between 1999 and 2009. About 30 percent of the time our youth use more than one media source at a time, such as listening to music while surfing the Web, which increases media exposure that kids experience during that 7.5-hour period.[10]

For years, some in the media have argued that exposure to sexual content does not affect the behavior of young people. Recent studies have put that argument where it belongs—in the trash heap of bad information. Multiple studies now link heavy exposure to sexual content in mainstream media with early sex, faster progression of sexual behaviors, sexually transmitted infections, and increased unplanned pregnancies.[11] One study, for example, shows that young people who indulge in a heavy diet of sexual content on TV are twice as likely as their peers who were not so exposed to engage in sexual intercourse.[12]

So now we know that our young people are inundated with a firehose-sized stream of sexually saturated media. We now know that, contrary to earlier arguments, this sexual content actually does result in more frequent sexual behavior. We will study the common results from this sexual involvement later, but suffice it to say that it can have devastating and lasting impacts.

Young people, particularly our daughters, are in crisis. They may not think they are—of course, adolescents rarely do. But the data are clear: They and their future are endangered. Parents who look away from their daughters' media use are doing them no favors. Instead of being helpful, broad-minded, and tolerant, in actuality these parents have abandoned their daughters just when their girls need them the most. They are leaving them uncovered and naked before this uncaring media onslaught and the people who stand ready to profit from it.

> If we don't give girls a reason to say no to guys who want to have sex, we leave them intellectually and morally defenseless.

The people who use these techniques to send dangerous messages to your daughter are often incredibly well funded, innovative, manipulative, and intelligent. They can present their messages in highly appealing forms that increase the likelihood of young people choosing to have sex. Your daughter is up against much. It is not fair for her to face it alone, even if she complains when you set limits or insist on being involved. Without your protection, she can and sometimes will be hurt horribly.

If we are not giving girls a reason to say no to guys who want to have sex with them, we are leaving them intellectually and morally defenseless. Without the hedge of protection that societies and parents have almost always provided, our girls are vulnerable to the desires of guys and even to their own inborn and newly awakening sexual interest.

In truth, the situation is even grimmer. We are not only disarming girls in the face of dangerous attacks on their personhood. We are actually allowing society to convince them that they should have sex if they are normal. Sometimes parents themselves contribute to this, an issue we will talk about later.

Here are some common assertions presented as "facts" that would cause most girls to ask, "Why *shouldn't* I have sex?" These "facts" have been popularized in a constant drumbeat across the culture. Some are commonly taught in school. Our youngsters, both male and female, hear them all the time, even before puberty. These "facts" are believed by most teens and college young people—and, perhaps most unfortunately of all, by many parents.

Remember that our girls are hearing these reasons to engage in sex in their seven or eight hours per day of sexually charged media use and in conversations with friends, teachers, and other adults. Keep in mind that as they hear these "facts," they are experiencing a constant bombardment of hormones and chemicals surging through their brains and bodies that arouse great interest in things sexual. (We will explore this topic in chapter 6, on emotional attachment.) All of these influences, internal and external, are driving them to believe the following:

Girls can use oral contraceptives, have intercourse, and not become pregnant.

If girls have intercourse without using oral contraceptives, they can use the "morning-after pill" or Ella, the new five-day emergency contraception product, and not become pregnant.

If girls become pregnant, they can just have an abortion. There is no downside to this minor procedure.

If girls become pregnant, it is their fault. They either failed to use "protection," or they used it incorrectly.

Girls can always get guys to use a condom.

If the guy uses a condom, there is no real risk of becoming infected with an STI (a sexually transmitted infection) or with HIV.

If the guy doesn't use a condom and the girl somehow becomes infected with an STI, it is her fault because she must not have insisted strongly enough.

If a girl does become infected, it is no big deal. All she has to do is see the doctor and get some antibiotics.

Girls should feel free to engage in sex the way they have heard that boys do—with anyone, anytime, anywhere, and with absolutely no regrets.

Girls should experience no downside to sexual encounters. They should expect nothing more out of sex than physical pleasure. If they do feel any emotional longing or regret, it means they have the problem. They must be too uptight, too naïve, or too religious. They should "get over it."

Everyone is "hooking up."

Girls can have sex without any emotional attachment to their partners.

Because girls are in control (except in cases of abuse), they can make an intellectual decision about whether or not to have sex.

If a girl is getting serious about a boyfriend, she should "take the car for a test drive." (In other words, this advice may range from *sexual activity to actually living together. Some say a girl should cohabit with a guy for a while to be sure they are compatible.)*

A girl can be strong and resist the urge to smoke, drink excessive alcohol, or use drugs. But the sex urge is so strong and inherently "natural" that it is unrealistic to think she can or should resist it.

Inevitably, girls will have sex before marriage.

Women and men are marrying so much later in life than they used to that it is unrealistic to think they can wait until marriage to have sex.

Happiness comes from living by your own progressive ideas and values, not by the conservative and outdated values of your parents or church.

Each of these supposed "facts" is false. We will expose them in the rest of this book. We will also show how they are extremely destructive to young women's capacity to make independent decisions about how to live. We will show how believing these deceptive messages has disempowered young women. We will show how misplaced belief has involved young women in sexual activity with devastating consequences for their physical and emotional health. In other words, we will show how society is leaving our young women uncovered, unprotected, vulnerable, and naked.

> *Making healthy choices can markedly increase girls' chances of achieving their full potential.*

But we will not leave it there. Concern is surely called for, but not depression! We will show how young women are not stupid, ignorant, witless pawns of sexual desire. We will show how, with guidance and encouragement, they can avoid destructive behaviors. We will show how making healthy choices can markedly increase girls' chances of achieving their full potential.

We want our young women to experience health, hope, and happiness. We know you want the same things for your daughter. We want to help you help them. So let's get started.

CHAPTER THREE

The Sexual Lives of Teens and Young Adults

JUST WHAT ARE TEENS and young adults in the United States doing with their bodies? Fortunately, ongoing research has provided solid answers to this question. Unfortunately, if you are like most parents, you will find the answers to be downright disturbing.

Vigen Guroian, a professor at Loyola College, quotes one of his female students:

> It may not be that dating is at the brink of extinction, but . . . it has taken a back seat in the modern-day lives of students. Hooking up, going out, going steady, and dating, contrary to what some may think, are not the same thing. . . . If you are "going out" with someone it means that you have a boyfriend or a girlfriend, you are in a "steady" relationship with that person. However, a couple needn't actually go anywhere [go on dates together] to be in this kind of relationship. Hooking up is basically dating without the romance. It has become customary for young adults to simply cut to the chase, the sexual . . . part of a relationship. A hookup can be a one-time thing, as it most often is, or it can be a semi-regular thing, but not a full relationship. Although it may take on the signs of one.

One might conclude that modern-day youth have simply gotten lazy and careless. Most . . . are not looking for a romantic relationship; they see the new freedom and plethora of sexual opportunities and simply take what they can get. They get to college, and it's an amusement park with so many different enticing rides, one would be missing out on the whole experience to settle with the first one they tried. And why should they bother with the responsibility and formalities of a date when they have a better chance of getting immediate satisfaction after buying a few drinks at a bar? . . .

> Become involved in guiding your daughter toward healthy values and behaviors, both for your girl's sake and for the good of the larger society.

Coed dormitories, are they an ideal situation or a sad form of prostitution? You go out with your friends on your terms, after a few drinks you're both attracted. . . . Interested and lonely, you go together, no obligations, no responsibilities, and no rules. Then there is that late-night "booty call." This has become such a custom of the college lifestyle [that] most have come to accept it, although maybe not respect it. If it were really the ideal situation, the walk home the next day [to one's own room] wouldn't be called "the walk of shame."[1]

Such a report from the university scene is disturbing, but parents need to grasp the predicament a daughter faces in her day-to-day life—or soon will face. As you understand the sexual behavior of today's youth, you can prepare yourself and your daughter for what is ahead. Knowing what is happening can serve as a wake-up call for you to become involved in guiding your daughter toward healthy values and behaviors, both for your girl's sake and for the good of the larger society.

The first thing you ought to know is that teens (up to the age of eighteen) and young adults (eighteen years of age and older) do not have the same levels of exposure to sexual activity. They face different challenges. The pressures for sexual involvement are much more intense for the older group. The good news is that you *may* have some critically needed time to prepare your precollege daughter for what lies ahead, when comparing her situation with that of a college student. It is still not a pretty picture, but any breathing room is good when it comes to protecting our daughters.

Realize that the numbers we are about to share come from scientific studies. You should give them a lot of credence, but understand that they do not represent your daughter's unalterable destiny. They provide a snapshot of what she may face or become, but they are not the final word. You will have much to say about her destiny, but you will be better equipped to do so by having these facts.

So here, first, are the facts about teen sexual activity. You can find reliable information in several places. One source is the Youth Risk Behavior Surveillance (YRBS) System, which monitors risky behavior among youth by administering surveys to thousands of students in public and private high schools across the US. Because this survey goes out every two years, researchers can track trends.[2]

Statistics do not represent your daughter's unalterable destiny.

Another source is the National Survey of Family Growth (NSFG). With the age of participants ranging from fifteen to forty-four years, the NSFG asks questions about sexual activity, marriage, pregnancy, and contraceptive use to thousands of men and women every year across the United States.[3] These studies provide some interesting insight into the sexual lives of teens.

According to the YRBS 2009 results, about 46 percent of high school girls have had sexual intercourse—nearly half. This is not uniform across all four high school years, however. Among ninth-grade girls, about 30 percent have had sex. If you think that number is too high, just wait. In tenth and eleventh grades, about 40 percent and 50 percent, respectively, report having had sex. In the twelfth grade, a full 65 percent report having had sex, and about 20 percent say that they have had *more than four partners*.[4]

So between freshman and senior years, the number of girls who have experienced intercourse more than doubles. Clearly, many girls are at risk of sexual involvement during high school. The good news is that you can still play a large role in helping your daughter to overcome this risk.

Up to now we have just mentioned intercourse, but you need to know that other forms of sexual activity, such as oral and anal sex, are also prevalent during high school. Some girls, in fact, choose these non-procreative forms of sexual activity in order to "save" their virginity and avoid the risk of pregnancy.

Oral sex is particularly popular, perhaps due to widespread misconceptions even about "what it is" and about the problems it might produce. First, many young people do not even consider oral sex to be sexual activity. Several research studies have asked undergraduate students if they would say that they "had sex" if they had participated in oral sex. Studies performed in 1991 and in 1999–2001 revealed that about 40 percent of college students classified oral sex as "sex." When a similar study was repeated in 2007, the results showed that only about 20 percent of college

> *We are witnessing a time when a generation's perspective on sexual behavior is actively changing.*

men and women considered oral sex to be "sex," a dramatic change from previous years.[5] If these research studies accurately reflect current societal beliefs, we are witnessing a time when a generation's perspective on sexual behavior is actively changing.

Another widespread misperception about oral sex is that it is risk-free. One study of college students revealed that fewer than 5 percent were concerned about STIs (sexually transmitted infections) after being involved in oral sex.[6] However, researcher Dr. Bonnie Halpern-Felsher states, "Oral sex is not risk free. There is evidence mounting that oral sex is associated with negative health outcomes such as STIs, including herpes, hepatitis, gonorrhea, chlamydia, syphilis, and HIV."[7] An amazing 40 percent or more of fifteen- to seventeen-year-olds participate in oral sex. Among eighteen-year-olds, a full 70 percent report having had oral sex.[8]

Anal sex, we are thankful to report, is not as prevalent among teens, but the inherent risks make it a major cause for concern anyway. Among fifteen- to seventeen-year-olds, only 5 percent report having had anal sex. Among eighteen-year-olds, the number is more worrisome, but it is still far lower than for oral sex: more than 18 percent.[9] That's not good at all, but it could be worse.

What about the sexual activities of young women aged eighteen and older? We have a host of data available. The National College Health Risk Behavior Surveillance, part of the YRBS study, is aimed exclusively at college students.[10] Another source of information is the American College Health Association's National College Health Assessment.[11] Drawing from these studies, we can start to put together a picture of the sexual behavior of these young women—and it is alarming.

Using NSFG results for American women aged twenty and twenty-one, more than 80 percent report having had vaginal sex. Just as many report having had oral sex, and more than 25 percent report having had anal sex.[12] Further, more than 25 percent of eighteen- to twenty-four-year-old college students report having had *six or more* sexual partners since becoming sexually active.[13] *And many of these college students are sexually active currently, with more than 40 percent reporting engaging in oral sex and vaginal sex in the past thirty days.*[14]

Clearly, sexual activity among teen girls and young women is common, presenting many risks to their physical and emotional health. Yet our daughters do not make these decisions in a vacuum. They don't just wake up one day and say, "I think I'll be sexually active." There are many reasons that today's girls and young women engage in acts their mothers and grandmothers would have found unthinkable at the same age. We cannot simply tell them these choices are wrong

> *Sexual activity among teen girls and young women is common, presenting many risks to their physical and emotional health.*

or unhealthy and they should "just say no" (though the choices *are* often not healthy). We need to understand and respond to the societal norms and expectations that influence young women's thinking and behavior.

A twenty-one-year-old woman came into Freda's office for an annual exam. In taking the woman's sexual history, Freda asked if she were in a relationship. The woman said no, not for nine months. Freda then asked her when she last engaged in intercourse, and she replied, "Two weeks ago." So Freda then asked the woman to clarify her two answers. The patient stated that she was not "in relationship" with her sexual partner from two weeks before. Freda then asked her to define what they were involved in. The twenty-one-year-old told Freda it was just a "physical thing."

So Freda asked her patient if she used condoms with her partners, and she answered, "Always." Then Freda asked if she had been "physical" with anyone else in the last nine months, and she said yes, with two others—and had used condoms with them, too. This patient thought that it was okay to have sex whenever she wanted as long as she used condoms every time.

Our daughters face a culture that sees sex as both a sacred right to be exercised with anyone, at any time, and also as "no big deal." As many observers of youth culture attest, this culture of "hooking up" among teens and young adults has come out of the closet. It has also become a topic of substantial research and deserves increased attention from parents.

Hooking up. What does that mean? Those who interview young people find that they define a "hookup" in a number of ways, but it usually indicates a sexual encounter that may or may not include intercourse.[15] Key elements actually involve what is *lacking*, at least from a traditional perspective on relations between the sexes. One significant characteristic is that romance frequently is not a part of the relationship; often two people have sex even though they have no preexisting romantic attachment. Another is the lack of expectation or obligation on the part of the participants for any future relationship. It is definitely a "no strings attached" approach to sexual activity between friends, acquaintances, or even complete strangers.[16] Tom Wolfe's 2004 novel, *I Am Charlotte Simmons*, painted a frightening picture of the convoluted sexual practices on college campuses that is actually quite realistic.

> *"Hooking up" indicates a sexual encounter that may or may not include intercourse.*

Seemingly in contrast to the hookup culture, the National Survey of Family Growth tells us that more than 70 percent of girls have sex for the first time with someone with whom they are in a committed relationship—either "going steady," cohabiting, engaged, or married.[17] But this relationship-oriented approach to sex doesn't last long for many girls and young women.

A large national survey of middle school and high school students who were followed over time illustrates the high occurrence of casual sexual encounters among teens. Most of these students engaged in sexual activity for the first time, as we said, with a girlfriend or boyfriend. However, within that same year, *75 percent* of these students also had sex with a casual partner.[18] Apparently having first sex in the context of a relationship is no defense against having casual sex later. In many cases, it seems to simply open the door to sexual relations with more people and denial of the unavoidable emotional consequences. (See chapter 6, "Emotional Attachment," for more information.)

In another study of more than a thousand teens in Ohio, more than 50 percent of the girls who were sexually active had engaged in sex outside of a romantic relationship. Most of these sexual encounters were with a friend, many with an ex-boyfriend.[19]

"Hooking up" can describe any sexually oriented activity, from kissing to intercourse. This includes being sexually stimulated or stimulating another person sexually. A term often used for this activity is mutual masturbation. Since this activity does not include penetration of the female, except perhaps by the fingers of a guy, many young people consider it safe. It is not. Several sexually transmitted infections can be spread by this activity, including syphilis. Perhaps more importantly, emotional issues can accompany this form of hooking up. Finally, most adults understand that mutual masturbation is no more than foreplay. A couple practicing this behavior will soon not be satisfied and will often progress to intercourse.

Hooking up is especially prevalent among college students. Some research shows that men and women have about twice as many hookups as first dates.[20] In one study, *78 percent* of college undergrads reported having participated in hookups, with a third of the women reporting that the hookup included intercourse.[21]

Young men and women agree about what happens in the typical hookup. Usually they:

- are at a bar or party where alcohol is being consumed;
- see a stranger or acquaintance whom they are attracted to;
- flirt or dance with this person;
- go to a private place;
- engage in sexual activity;
- then leave without future obligation.[22]

College students believe this is normal heterosexual behavior—and, unfortunately, it has indeed become "normal," as the statistics we have shown suggest. Karen Owen, a recent graduate of Duke University, sparked a national sensation when a PowerPoint of her sexual encounters with thirteen athletes at Duke went viral. Even some of today's feminists were aghast at such openness about sexual behavior.

Caitlyn Flanagan of *The Atlantic* writes, "We've made a culture for our college women in which they have been liberated from the curfews and parietals that were once the bane of coeds, but one in which they have also shaken off the general suspicion of male sexuality that was the hallmark of Andrea Dworkin–style campus activism; they prefer bikini waxes and spray tans to overalls and invective. So they have ended up with the protections of neither the patriarchy nor those old-school, man-hating radical feminists."[23]

Yet the growing prevalence of this behavior apparently rests at least partly on a misperception. Research shows that both male and female college students actually *overestimate* their classmates' comfort level with hooking up. While large numbers of young people may be uncomfortable with hooking up, many mistakenly believe that they are in the minority when they feel doubt and discomfort. When asked to compare their comfort level with that of their male and female peers on campus, young women believe, on average, that others feel more comfortable with hooking up than they do. Some female college students report that they drink alcohol with the intention of loosening their very natural inhibitions to hooking up.[24]

Alcohol consumption, not surprisingly, plays a large part in the hookup culture. Alcohol is a standard part of the hookup in many college students' minds. One study shows that more than 80 percent of hookups involve alcohol,[25] while another indicates that more than 90 percent of college students expect alcohol to be involved in hookups.[26]

Alcohol seems to play a major role in the sexual involvement of young people. Nearly one-fourth of sexually active high school students report using drugs or alcohol during their most recent sexual experience,[27] and nearly one in five teens said that they were under the influence of drugs or alcohol when they had sex for the first time.[28] In one study of college women, 23 percent reported a history of unwanted sexual intercourse. Of those incidents, 78 percent took place while "hooking up." When the women were asked about the factors that contributed to the unwanted sexual intercourse, 62 percent said that their "judgment was impaired by alcohol or drugs" and 32 percent said that they were taken advantage of while they were drunk.[29] Clearly, substance abuse affects a person's ability to make judgments about sexual behavior, thus increasing the risk for pregnancy, sexual assault, and sexually transmitted infections.

However, alcohol and hooking up are not the only societal currents pulling our daughters in the wrong directions. We briefly mentioned another new activity, this one enabled by today's technology, called "sexting." Sexting involves young people using technology such as cell phones and the Internet to send sexually suggestive messages or nude/seminude pictures of themselves to others. Unfortunately, many of them also see this behavior as entirely "normal."

Although media reports about the terrible consequences of "sexting" have made parents more aware of how it can put girls and young women at risk, most are probably unaware that their own daughter may be participating. And national statistics tell us that many of these daughters *are*! Are you among the masses of parents comfortably believing your daughter couldn't possibly be involved?

> About two-thirds of teen girls will have had sex by the time they graduate from high school.

Think again. The National Campaign to Prevent Teen and Unplanned Pregnancy teamed with *cosmogirl.com* on a 2008 survey of nearly 1,300 teens and young adults about sexting. Among the results:

- 22 percent of 13- to 19-year-old girls responding to the survey say they have electronically sent or posted nude or seminude pictures of themselves.
- 36 percent of 20- to 26-year-olds admit to doing the same.

• 37 percent of 13- to 19-year-olds and 56 percent of 20- to 26-year-olds say they have sent or posted sexually suggestive messages.[30]

The prevalence of sexting among both teens and young adults speaks to one potential negative impact of technology and the need for adult supervision and guidance. Without parental input, young people can quickly get in over their heads. In one well-publicized case, six high school teens in Greensburg, Pennsylvania, faced child pornography charges after three girls shared nude or seminude photos of themselves with male classmates via cell phone.[31] While that may be an unusual example, it shows what can happen.

The sexualized nature of our culture has a huge influence on our daughters, especially as they pass through high school and college. About two-thirds of them will have had sex by the time they graduate from high school—both within a romantic relationship and a casual partnership. By the time they graduate from college, the vast majority of these young women will have had sex. Many will have participated in high-risk behaviors, including having:

> *Going against the grain of popular culture is difficult for anyone, but it is especially hard for young people.*

• multiple partners,
• a partner with multiple partners,
• sex under the influence of drugs or alcohol,
• anal sex, or
• oral sex.

Many parents, and perhaps you as well, will find this information frightening—and rightly so. These statistics illustrate how toxic the environment is for our daughters. For those who want to swim against the tide and maintain their virginity until marriage, it seems that every influence is against them. Our daughters have high educational and career goals, yet we see how difficult it is for them to stay focused on their studies and not to be drawn into sexual distraction and involvement. And of course the same can be said for those who have high family goals of being married, having children, and staying married.

Going against the grain of popular culture is difficult for anyone. But it is especially hard for young people, who are so conscious of trends, fashion, and peers. The data we have highlighted show the negative consequences inherent in sexual involvement outside of a lifelong, faithful relationship. They show how such involvement threatens the lives and potentials of many teen girls and *most* young women —even yours. We would like to think our own daughters are not at risk, but the statistics presented in this chapter counsel vigilance. Therefore, you must not only be concerned about your daughter's well-being through these formative years. You must also be prepared to guide her through the tough decisions and perplexing situations that she will likely face.

A girl uncovered is a girl at risk.

In the next chapter, we will take an unflinching look at some of the most immediate and measurable negative consequences of sexual activity among youth—sexually transmitted infections. We are not including this information to scare you or your daughter. We simply want to arm you with the facts so that you and your daughter can more realistically discuss wise sexual choices.

Parenting is not for the faint of heart or the uninvolved. If you want to protect and support your daughter, it will cost you—in terms of time, money, effort, even relational pain. But think of this as a calling, and the costs as investments—because the payoff in the life of your daughter could be huge. No, there are no guarantees, but we believe your daughter has a much better likelihood of surviving and thriving during these difficult years if you stay engaged and provide the "cover" she so desperately needs. For a girl uncovered is a girl at risk.

CHAPTER FOUR

STIs

JOE SAW A YOUNG WOMAN for infertility. She and her husband had been trying to become pregnant for three years. Joe performed the usual preliminary tests, such as a sperm count, and found nothing wrong—except that the X-ray of her fallopian tubes suggested blockage.

Joe did a laparoscopy, which is the insertion of a viewing instrument through an incision in the edge of her umbilicus. What he saw immediately revealed why she could not get pregnant. Her internal female organs looked as though someone had poured glue all over them. Her fallopian tubes were not only blocked by extensive scarring, they were stuck to her ovaries. Also, her ovaries and tubes were stuck to some of her intestines and to her uterus. In short, her female organs were an inoperable mess of scar tissue.

What caused all this? The woman had been a flight attendant before marriage and had been sexually involved with several men. She had become infected with an STI but had never felt a thing. But the damage was real—and irreversible. Joe saw this situation over and over again; all infertility doctors do.

Do teens and young adults really know the risks involved with all of the sexual activity that they report? Do they have any idea about the STIs they may encounter? They may *think* they know the risks. Between 85 and 90 percent of high school students say they have been taught in school about HIV/AIDS.[1] And more than 50 percent of college students say that they have received STI information from their college or university.[2] So

35

most of these young people would say that they have been educated about STIs, including HIV.

If education is so prevalent, then why do so many take part in risky sexual behavior, such as hookups? In one recent study, only about 50 percent of college students who reported having intercourse during a hookup said that they were concerned about getting an STI. And of those who had oral sex during the hookup, less than 50 percent were worried about a possible STI.[3]

STIs are very common among teens and young adults, and they have the potential to change a young person's life forever.

When the college students were asked why they were not concerned about getting an STI, two answers were common: (1) they trusted that their partners were "clean" because they were acquainted with them and knew something about their previous relationships; and (2) they felt their community had a low rate of HIV infections. After talking with the students, the researchers concluded that the students did not understand the true STI risk, especially with oral sex.[4]

The truth is, STIs are very common among teens and young adults, and they have the potential to change a young person's life forever. Just how common? In the US in the year 2000, an estimated 19 million cases of sexually transmitted infections occurred. About half of these infections occurred in fifteen- to twenty-four-year-olds, even though they only represent about 25 percent of the sexually active population.[5]

For example, one study showed that in a period of eighteen months, more than 50 percent of students at a certain high school were chained together through romantic and sexual relationships that could have involved the exchange of fluids. (This means that one student had had sex with another, who had had sex with another, thus creating a "chain" of contacts.) This behavior is one of the most efficient ways of transmitting disease. Almost 35 percent of the students (189) were part of isolated partnerships. In this case, the partners had no other sex partners before or after the relationship.[6]

We are mainly addressing girls and young women and their parents in this book, and one of the primary reasons is that girls are so much more frequently *severely affected* by STIs. We will give example after example. For instance, one of the saddest results of an STI is infertility.[7] Many young women aged fifteen to twenty-four have not started having a family yet, and so the infertility that can result from an STI is particularly devastating. Further, the immaturity of the cervix of girls through their teen years makes them more vulnerable to infection and cervical cancer (which is almost always due to an STI). Therefore, teen girls and young women have a lot to lose when it comes to STIs. Let's examine some of the important STIs.

Teen girls and young women have a lot to lose when it comes to STIs.

First, let's address the term "STI." An STI is an infection usually spread by sexual contact. Many people use the term STD, or sexually transmitted *disease*, rather than STI. We use STI because many of these infections do not cause symptoms, and so many infected people do not think that they have a "disease." However, when people have an infection, with or without disease symptoms, not only may their bodies face the prospect of damage, but they are also capable of spreading that infection to their sexual partners. Therefore, we will use the term STI throughout this book.

HPV

One of the very common STIs among young people is human papillomavirus, or HPV. HPV can be extremely contagious. It is probably spread in about one of every two sex acts when one partner is infected and the other partner is not.[8]

There are more than a hundred types of HPV. About forty infect the genital area, while the other 60 percent cause problems such as finger warts or plantar warts. Of the types that cause genital infection, about half are called "high risk" because they are known to cause cervical cancer.[9, 10] The others are called "low risk" because they do not usually cause cancer. Instead, the low-risk types cause genital warts.

HPV infections are very common among youth, with the infections often acquired in their first sexual experience.[11] About 25 percent of teen girls and about 45 percent of twenty- to twenty-four-year-old women have a genital HPV infection.[12] And levels of infection may be even higher among men.[13] Therefore, it is estimated that about 75 percent of the US population will eventually be infected by HPV.[14]

Genital HPV infections may even be found among girls who have not had sexual intercourse. The human papillomavirus is present on the skin of infected genitalia and can spread through skin-to-skin contact, possibly even by hand-to-genital contact.[15] Therefore, even girls who participate in sexual activities not usually considered "sex," such as heavy petting, may be at risk for HPV infection.

There is no cure for HPV, because it is a virus, although the body's natural immune system will usually clear an HPV infection within two years.[16] Approximately 10 percent of people do not clear the HPV infection within this period of time and are at risk for chronic warts or various cancers, especially cervical cancer in women. There are many treatments available for warts and precancerous or cancerous lesions, but there is no cure for the underlying infection. HPV is not only associated with cervical cancer, but also with cancer of the vagina, penis, anus, and head/neck.[17]

As disturbing as these facts about HPV are, they do not tell the excruciating story of what it is like to develop the warts or the abnormal Pap smear that can result from an HPV infection. We both have seen the anxiety in hundreds of patients we have treated for these infections. It is painful for a physician to see the surprise and even anger when informing the patient that the little bump just found on her vulva is a wart caused by a sexually transmitted virus.

Adolescent patients often become fearful when we tell them their very abnormal Pap smear is probably caused by a sexually transmitted virus. They especially hate experiencing the pain of the doctor using an instrument to cut small pieces off their cervix to make sure no cancer is present.

A young woman came to Joe for an annual exam and Pap smear. She had been married for a year. Unfortunately, her husband had had many sexual partners before they were married. While her premarital Pap smear had been normal, this one showed signs of developing cancer. Colposcopy (magnifying the cervix through a viewing instrument) and biopsies were done. These tests showed that some of the cells of the cervix had almost developed into cancer and required that more of the cervical tissue be removed. Fortunately, this solved the problem. However, this couple soon divorced as a result of the husband's severe emotional problems.

It is women who suffer most of the problems related to STIs.

Less than a year later, however, he brought another woman to the office. Another doctor had found cells on her cervix that were almost cancer. Joe looked at the reports and verified that they were accurate. More of her cervix had to be removed to prevent her from developing invasive cancer. This procedure requires stitches in the cervix. Occasionally the stitches will pull through the tissues and cause heavy bleeding. This happened, unfortunately, to the second woman. She had to rush back to the office to have more stitches put in—not a comfortable procedure!

Clearly it is women who suffer most of the problems related to STIs. In this case, the man was carrying a very dangerous strain of HPV on his penis and passing it to women. He ended up causing *them* to suffer the problems from his HPV infection.

At the start of this discussion, we mentioned that HPV is very common. The numbers are staggering, and every teen, young adult, and parent should ponder them. HPV infection in women leads to about 3.5 million abnormal Pap smears

Parents can understand how future problems can derive from actions taken today.

every year in the US.[18] Every one of these abnormal tests then needs to be followed up by more tests. In some cases, this means a colposcopy and cervical biopsy.[19]

The tests that follow an abnormal Pap smear usually cause stress, fear, and pain for the young women subjected to them. If the biopsies show severe precancerous or cancerous changes, then the lesions must be removed from the cervix. This type of surgery may be necessary to keep cancer from developing or progressing. Even though doctors will perform this procedure with the utmost care, the cervix can still be damaged enough to produce problems later in life, such as infertility or premature labor if pregnancy does occur.

The problem, of course, is that it is difficult for a teenage girl, or even a young woman, to think about potential problems years in the future when she is considering or involved in sexual activity now. This is one reason parents are so important in a young person's life. Parents are better able to understand how future problems can derive from actions taken today

One of the saddest experiences of a gynecologist's life is to see a woman die from cervical cancer. Each of us has seen that happen. And, sadly, approximately 275,000 women worldwide[20] (more than 5,200 in the United States[21]) die of cervical cancer every year. Many of these deaths could have been prevented by these women and the guys they cared about if they had committed to a lifelong monogamous relationship.

Unfortunately, HPV does not just cause cervical cancer. It is linked to vaginal and vulvar cancer, as well as anal cancer and cancer of the inside of the mouth and throat (and these oral cancers have been increasing in younger people in the past few years).[22] And it may play a key role in even more cancers.[23, 24, 25] It is easy to see, then, how spreading HPV through oral sex and anal sex can also be dangerous to young women.

Finally, though genital warts are not dangerous, they can be excruciating. Their treatment requires medication that can cause a burning discomfort of the vulva. Though many times, one or two treatments will cause the warts to go away, this is not always the case. Sometimes treatment requires many visits to the doctor. Young women find the entire experience agonizing. Unfortunately, it happens thousands of times every day.

HPV vaccines have the potential to significantly reduce HPV infections and thus the associated risk. Vaccines against measles, mumps, rubella, and tetanus have been recommended and given in childhood for decades, as recommended by the Advisory Committee on Immunization Practices (ACIP). Now, recent scientific advances have made available two vaccines to prevent some HPV infection. These vaccines provide immunity against four common HPV types: 16, 18, 6, and 11. Scientific evidence on immunization with one of the vaccines suggests that it substantially reduces the risk of precancer and cancer of the cervix caused by HPV types 16 and 18[26] (responsible for about 70 percent of all cervical cancers in the US[27]). Additionally, evidence on a second vaccine suggests that it substantially reduces the risk caused by HPV types 16 and 18 and HPV types 6 and 11[28] (responsible for about 90 percent of all genital warts in the US[29]). The Advisory Committee on Immunization Practices recommends these vaccines be given beginning ages eleven and twenty-six for girls and young women.[30]

Regarding vaccines, the Medical Institute, a nonprofit research organization that provides scientific information on sexual health, supports regular but not mandatory vaccination against HPV for adolescent girls. Regular health screening and counseling are important, including pelvic examinations and Pap smear screening. The recommendations for the frequency of Pap smear screenings have changed with our understanding of the nature of HPV, which causes most of the abnormal Pap smear findings and may be cleared by the body within two (or even three) years. It is important that women check with their physicians or practitioners about particular health concerns and risks.

Risk factors for HPV infection are:

- Young age (peak age group: 20–24),[31]
- Lifetime high number of sex partners,[32]

- Early age of first sexual intercourse,[33]
- Male partner sexual behavior,[34]
- Smoking,[35]
- Oral contraceptive use,[36]
- Uncircumcised male partners.[37]

Girls and young women need to understand the risk factors of HPV so they can avoid it.

Chlamydia

The most commonly reported bacterial STI is chlamydia. More than 1 million cases are reported every year in the US.[38] And these are just the infections diagnosed by the medical system and reported to the government. When you take into account all of the infections that go undiagnosed, an estimated 1.5 million new cases of chlamydia infection occur every year in fifteen- to twenty-four-year-olds alone.[39]

Unfortunately, the group with the highest rate of chlamydia infection is fifteen- to nineteen-year-old girls, followed closely by twenty- to twenty-four-year-old women.[40] The immaturity of the cervix in teen girls may be the reason. The cells covering the cervix change over time, with a tougher layer of cells growing over the cervix as girls move from their teens into their twenties or after they deliver a baby. The immature cervix appears to be particularly susceptible to chlamydia.

Up to 90 percent of females with a chlamydia infection do not recognize any symptoms.[41] Without symptoms, many do not think of going to their health care provider to be checked for an STI, no matter what their sexual activity has been. If a chlamydia infection is diagnosed in a female, it is usually easy to treat with a prescription for oral antibiotics. If, however, the chlamydia infection is not treated quickly enough, it can spread through the reproductive tract and cause pelvic inflammatory disease or PID. PID causes scarring and other damage in and around the fallopian tubes, setting the stage for infertility, ectopic pregnancies, and chronic pelvic pain.

Although antibiotics can treat the chlamydia infection and prevent further damage, they cannot reverse the effects that have already taken place as a result of PID. After one episode of PID, about 8 percent of women will become infertile. After three episodes of PID, about 40 percent of women will become infertile.[42] Obviously, chlamydia, the most commonly reported bacterial STI, is a common and harmful infection for young women.

There are so many dangers for young women from chlamydia that you might think we are exaggerating. Believe us, we are not. Joe is an infertility specialist, involved in the care of infertile couples for many years. He has done laparoscopy, microsurgery, and IVF hundreds of times. Many of his patients required his care because the woman had been infected with chlamydia when in high school or college. Almost none had known of the infection. Almost none were aware that their sexual involvement when young could result in infertility later.

The broken hearts we see when the fertility treatments do not work is hard to describe—especially in young people, many of whom are looking forward to what they consider the biggest and most exciting parts of their lives. They can't imagine anything interfering with the future. They just don't grasp the very real danger of chlamydia. Let us repeat: Girls and young women who are sexually involved can become infected with chlamydia and not know it. Chlamydia can damage their fallopian tubes without their having *any* idea they are infected. They may not find out for years.

The Centers for Disease Control recommends that all women who are sexually active and under the age of twenty-five be tested every year for chlamydia.[43] But this recommendation has obvious limits. If a girl gets tested today but has sex with a guy tomorrow and he infects her with chlamydia, she may be infected for a year before the annual test reveals it. In the meantime, the infection might make her infertile, a condition she might not discover for years.

We emphasize again that though infertility treatments are available, they are extremely expensive. They:

- are emotionally taxing,
- are time and schedule taxing,
- are physically taxing (often requiring multiple injections and surgery),
- can be very financially taxing (and don't always work),
- can be morally taxing.

Many couples agonize over spending their resources on infertility care or in vitro fertilization. Because of such stringent financial demands, many couples are never able to pursue infertility care all the way to becoming pregnant. Certainly adoption is available and is a wonderful experience for many infertile couples. But young women usually expect to physically carry their own children in their own uterus, and infertility can remove that choice.

Gonorrhea

In many ways, gonorrhea is like chlamydia. Although it is not as common as chlamydia, gonorrhea still causes an estimated 430,000 infections per year in fifteen- to twenty-four-year-olds.[44] And, in the same hidden manner as chlamydia, as many as 85 percent of these infections do not cause symptoms.[45] Without symptoms, many girls do not know that they are infected and need to seek medical care.

Gonorrhea is usually easy to treat with oral antibiotics. But in cases where it is not diagnosed or treated, the infection can rise through the reproductive tract, causing PID. As we discussed with regard to chlamydia, the long-term effects of PID can include infertility, ectopic pregnancies, and chronic pelvic pain.

And, like chlamydia, the highest rates of gonorrhea infection are found among girls aged fifteen to nineteen, followed by young women aged twenty to twenty-four.[46] Because gonorrhea is so common among young women, the long-term effects of untreated infection, like infertility, can be especially devastating.

Genital Herpes

In the early days of his practice, Joe worked part-time at the student health center of a local university. One day a young woman student hobbled into the office, crying. When Joe examined her genital area, he found the reason for her pain and tears. She had one of the worst cases of herpes infection he had ever seen. Her entire vulva was covered with ugly ulcers. They were so excruciating that she could not urinate. Her distended bladder added to her pain.

Joe admitted her to the health center hospital, inserted a catheter into her bladder, and started her on medication. The next day, another young woman entered the health center with exactly the same painful symptoms. He put her in the hospital, put a catheter in her bladder, and gave her medication. When Joe came around at the end of the day to see how these young women were doing, they sheepishly admitted that they had both had sex with a rock star who had played at the university the weekend before—another example of the man carrying the STI and the woman suffering from it.

Genital herpes is caused by the herpes simplex virus, or HSV. HSV-1 has traditionally been considered the cause of oral herpes, also known as "fever blisters" or "cold sores." HSV-2 has traditionally been considered the cause of genital herpes. Recent research, however, has shown that both types can, and frequently do, cause genital herpes. In the past, physicians were not too concerned about patients having "fever blisters" on their lips. However, now that we know HSV-1 can also infect the genital region, physicians are concerned about the risk of oral sex. "Fever blisters" can cause a genital herpes infection to the person receiving the oral sex.

An estimated 640,000 new cases of genital herpes infections occur in fifteen- to twenty-four-year-olds every year.[47] Of these, only about 20 percent will develop ulcers in their genital regions.[48] Although the other 80 percent may not recognize any symptoms of a herpes infection, all of them will remain infected for life. Even if none of the painful ulcers appears, an infected person can spread the virus to sexual partners. Also, because the virus can spread through the bloodstream and through the nervous system, infected individuals may have other, unrecognized symptoms.

One of our associates, an infectious disease specialist, remembers treating a patient who had been hospitalized with multiple episodes of meningitis. The lab found HSV-2 in a sample of his spinal fluid. This physician told him that the likely cause of repeated episodes of meningitis was the herpes virus in his spinal fluid, which had probably resulted from a previous genital herpes infection (once on the genitals, herpes can, rarely, spread through the bloodstream to other parts of the body). The patient told our associate that this could not be right. The patient knew what genital herpes looked like and had never seen anything like that on his body. But the truth is that most people who have been infected with the virus don't know they have been infected.

An estimated one in six American adults is infected with HSV-2.[49] One reason herpes infection is so common is that there is *no cure*. Once people are infected, they are infected *for life*. Yes, certain medicines can help reduce the *length* of the outbreaks of genital ulcers or limit the *number* of outbreaks, but there is no cure for any human virus, and this one remains in the body.

Except for occasional dangerous complications, such as meningitis, or newborn babies becoming infected during pregnancy or delivery, the problems of herpes are primarily emotional. A person who becomes infected can feel that a sexual partner has violated a trust: "The person who infected me must have known that he had herpes but didn't bother to tell me." Actually, this may or may not be true; many infected people do not know they are infected, though of course many do.

The fact is, people who become infected, if they are knowledgeable, know they are infected for life. An infected person may have outbreaks of herpes blisters, unless taking suppressive medication, for many years, some even for the rest of their lives. Infected people must deal with the fact that they can infect any future sexual partners, including any "hookups" but also their future spouses.

Any infected woman must deal with the fact that she can pass her infection to her newborn baby either during pregnancy or at delivery—and when this happens, some of the babies will die and some will be brain-damaged. Yes, the risk is extremely small, but it is real. Is it any wonder that at least one study shows that more than half the people with initial genital herpes infection experience psychological symptoms, including anxiety,[50] and many feel stigmatized and distressed?[51] Many of these symptoms go away if there are no further herpes recurrences. But, in the cases of repeated herpes outbreaks, these psychological problems can continue for a long time.[52]

In order for young people to enjoy lives as free of burdens in the future as possible, freedom from herpes is a goal worth having.

HIV/AIDS

Though in some sense we are no longer shocked by it, the human immunodeficiency virus (HIV), which caused so much fear and gained so much media coverage in the 1980s, continues to be a formidable opponent for patients, doctors, and researchers. Because there is still no cure for the viral infection, and no vaccine, HIV/AIDS remains a dreaded diagnosis.

HIV infection usually causes symptoms in its earliest stages. But because they look similar to symptoms of mononucleosis or the flu, most people do not recognize what they signify. It is only years later, often up to a decade later, that infected individuals recognize the symptoms of advanced HIV infection. However, during all of the intervening years, the HIV virus was in the body, reproducing itself and destroying the immune system—and putting others at risk. It is usually only when the immune system becomes badly damaged that infected individuals learn that they have HIV.

An infectious disease specialist who consulted with us relates the story of a woman in her thirties who had recently been married, who was brought to the hospital by her husband because she was complaining of severe headaches. He had noticed that she was not thinking clearly. The physician soon determined that the underlying cause of her severe symptoms was a previously unknown HIV infection that had destroyed her immune system. It had allowed cervical cancer to develop and rapidly metastasize to her head. Decreased immunity can allow cancer to spread more rapidly. She died within days, because of previously undiagnosed HIV and HPV infections.

If this woman had been diagnosed sooner, she could have taken medicines to help control the virus and allow the immune system to partially repair itself. Consistent treatment with HIV medicines can extend an infected person's life for years, even decades. But no medicine can *cure* HIV, at least not yet. The medicines available to fight HIV have to be taken every day without fail. HIV medicines are very expensive and frequently cause side effects, but if a patient stops taking them for any reason, the virus has the opportunity to build up resistance to those medicines.

Currently, we have a very limited selection of HIV medicines. Once an HIV-infected person has been exposed to different HIV medicines, his or her HIV virus may become resistant to most or all of them. A resistant HIV infection that cannot be controlled with medicine can replicate quickly and overwhelm the immune system. When this happens, the infected person will develop AIDS, the final (and usually fatal) stage of HIV infection. Unfortunately, no vaccine has been developed to prevent HIV infection, despite years of effort.

We must educate our young people about HIV. Some of them think that HIV is so rare that they will never encounter it through sex with the people they know. This is not the case. Recent statistics reveal that there are more than 56,000 new HIV infections in the US every year. More than 30 percent of these occur as a result of heterosexual contact.[53] It is estimated that one in every fifty-three males will be diagnosed with HIV during his lifetime.[54]

Freda had a twenty-one-year-old patient referred by an infectious disease specialist for gynecology care. This young woman had been diagnosed as HIV-positive by a free health screening at a local college. Her sexual history revealed she was now married and had one previous relationship, in high school. It seems her first partner was a "closet" intravenous drug user—and she had acquired the HIV from him. Of course she wondered, "What if I had waited for marriage?"

Clearly, HIV is a large and far-reaching problem that affects thousands and thousands of people, leaving many sexually active youth vulnerable.

Young people might erroneously think that since "medicine" for HIV exists, it is no big deal if they become infected. They reason that whenever they got sick as children they simply took some medicine and were fine. How much different could an HIV infection be? They need to know that taking the "medicine" for HIV is very different from whatever else they may have taken. Taking HIV medications will control their lives. They must take them precisely, on time, every day, or they risk seeing their virus rapidly become resistant. Often the medicine is toxic and causes nausea or diarrhea. And it is very expensive. It is not unusual for the medicine to cost $15,000 to $20,000 a year.[55]

Then infected persons live with the knowledge that anytime they have sex, they may infect others. This is a very, very heavy burden. Also, an infected woman must live with the fact that unless she has excellent medical care throughout her pregnancy, she could pass the infection to any baby she might deliver. So, whether pregnant or not, an infected woman will be constantly visiting, consulting with, and being treated by medical professionals. One could almost say that her life will no longer be her own.

Syphilis

Syphilis has afflicted many important and influential people in Europe and America since the fifteenth century—and it is still dangerous in the twenty-first century. When penicillin became widely available after World War II, the incidence of syphilis fell from about 485,000 cases in 1941 to about 35,000 cases in 1999. In part due to the dramatic decline, the CDC developed a plan in 1999 to eradicate syphilis by the year 2005.[56] Unfortunately, after an all-time low rate of reported syphilis infections in 2000, infection rates in the US began to rise again. While rates of early syphilis are about five times higher in men than in women, rates among women are rising, too.[57]

Syphilis infection results from direct contact with the bacteria. Often an ulcer, called a chancre, is the first sign of the infection. Because the ulcer is painless and heals on its own, many people do not go to a health care provider to be checked for an STI. The untreated infection spreads throughout the body, causing a rash and flu-like symptoms for a short time. The person remains infectious for about a year, after which the bacteria remain in the body without spreading to sexual partners.

There are more than twenty-five STIs altogether.

After many years, an untreated syphilis infection can damage blood vessels, nerves, the brain, or other parts of the body, causing long-term symptoms and, possibly, death. When syphilis is finally diagnosed, penicillin is an effective treatment. But the damage that the infection has already caused to the body may be permanent.

Other Considerations

There are more than twenty-five STIs altogether,[58] and they are responsible for a marked decline in the health and well-being of American youth. As we have seen, STIs cause a significant amount of physical harm to girls and young women (and even older women). They also cause an immeasurable amount of emotional harm, with infected girls wondering about how an STI will affect their future relationships and achievements and with uninfected girls worrying how they will avoid STIs.

There are a few additional points that deserve your consideration. Most of the STIs we have examined can increase a person's chance of acquiring HIV from an HIV-infected partner. Also, each of these STIs can be passed to a baby, whether before, during, or after birth. Indeed, syphilis, herpes, and HIV can be fatal to a baby, emphasizing the far-reaching impact—even to the next generation—of STIs in our girls and young women.

And here's another point: The pain associated with many STIs may last for a long time. Both the authors of this book have cared for women who dealt with pain, anger, and shame related to their STIs every time they had a recurrence of their genital warts or herpes. It is heartbreaking to hear how they feel betrayed by the partners who gave them the infections and ashamed of telling future partners of their infections. The pent-up anger and pain that accompany these infections, along with other STIs, can be overwhelming.

And one final point to consider: Many STIs cause more problems for females than for males. We will make the point again in this book that "sex is sexist," placing a larger burden on women than on men. This certainly appears to be the case for STIs. While HPV causes cancer in both men and women, women are, by far, the most affected, with more than 12,000 cases of invasive cervical cancer occurring every year in the US.[59]

> *Sex is sexist, placing a larger burden on women than on men.*

Gonorrhea and chlamydia infections behave similarly. Men and women may both experience illness from these infections, but the long-term consequences of PID are primarily experienced by women, who then must deal with the pain—emotional and physical—of permanently damaged reproductive tracts.

Because the long-term effects of STIs fall on girls more than on guys, they are also the ones who are usually exposed to the screening tests. It is recommended that women get regular Pap smears to monitor for the effects of HPV on the cervix. Women's warts, if they get them, can be difficult to eradicate and may require many visits to the doctor. (Warts for men are usually quickly treated because male genitals do not provide as welcoming an environment for the virus.)

In the case of herpes, it is the woman who feels the horrible, burning pain of her genitals when first infected. The pain is sometimes so severe that she cannot urinate. In the case of chlamydia, it is the female who is advised to be tested every year if she is sexually active. It is the woman who, when she is pregnant, must undergo testing and treatment for any STI she might be infected with for the good of the baby.

Once Joe saw a young woman from one of the wealthiest families in town. She came because of itching in her vulvar area. Joe quickly found genital lice, which are sometimes called "crabs" because of their appearance. They were crawling all through her genital hair. Though they don't cause any physical damage, they provoke a great deal of stress and cause almost any woman to feel "dirty."

This woman told Joe that she had recently had sex with a new guy. During her next office visit, she said that the guy admitted he had gone across the border from Texas into Mexico and had engaged in sex with a prostitute.

This unbalanced nature of the effects of sexual activity may not seem fair—facts are often hard things—but this is reality. STIs present a complicated world of problems. As we shall see later, there is no sure way for girls and young women to avoid these problems if they are sexually active.

Educate your daughter and help her avoid sexual involvement until she settles down with one person for life.

It's a proven fact that condoms are not adequate protection.[60] In spite of all the years of medical research, nothing else exists to make such sexual involvement safe.

Unless you educate your daughter and help her avoid sexual involvement until she settles down with one person for life, you are leaving her naked and exposed to all of these potential problems.

CHAPTER FIVE

Pregnancy

WE HAVE SEEN the pervasiveness of STIs. Though they affect a large proportion of teens and young adults, STIs never attract much attention. Our silence makes the epidemic all the more dangerous, because we and our daughters do not grasp the risks of sexual activity. From television and popular culture, parents and children receive few reminders of how frequently these problems affect sexually active teens.

The issue of teen and nonmarital pregnancy is different, however. The pregnancy that comes to a husband and wife, of course, usually brings joy. But pregnancy among teens and the unmarried can produce feelings of grief, panic, shame, and bewilderment.

Unlike STIs, pregnancy sooner or later comes out in the open. Symptoms usually occur relatively quickly. A pregnant girl will miss her period, experience breast tenderness, feel sick, and have many of the other usual indicators. And it isn't long before parents and others around her begin to notice.

Out-of-wedlock pregnancy also brings unique family issues. The children our unmarried daughters have will be our grandchildren, whether they are adopted out or not. And our daughter and we all will become tied to the biological father—whether we want this relationship or not. The resulting complexity of relationships can have recurring stresses, especially as children mature and may want to know about biological parents—or even to know them personally. Many unpleasant memories can accompany disclosure about biological parents. Avoiding the potential of

In the United States, every year about 750,000 teen girls get pregnant.

such painful baggage is one of the reasons parents focus on ensuring that their daughters do not get pregnant in the first place.

In the United States, every year about 750,000 teen girls get pregnant, leading to more than 430,000 births and more than 200,000 abortions.[1] It is estimated that about *three in ten* girls will get pregnant by the time they turn twenty.[2] That statistic is frightening. Most girls under age twenty, and their parents, acknowledge that they are not ready to be pregnant nor prepared to deal with the consequences. And the consequences for the teen mother and her child are significant.

A group of researchers has spent many years trying to demonstrate the true impact of teen pregnancy and childbearing on our society. In the book *Kids Having Kids: Economic Costs & Social Consequences of Teen Pregnancy*, these researchers compiled one of the most exhaustive analyses ever attempted.[3] They looked at the effects on the teen mother, child, and father individually and compared them to outcomes for families with a mother who is slightly older, often aged twenty or twenty-one. They tried to take into account the education and other social circumstances of the mother in order to determine which consequences could be attributed to the mere age of the mother and father at the time of a birth. The sobering results should serve as a warning to parents who hope that their children will move into adulthood unencumbered, free to achieve their goals.

Several disadvantages to the teen mother quickly become apparent. For one, teen mothers spend, on average, about five times longer as single parents from the time they are fourteen to the time they are thirty than women who delay childbearing until after their teenage years. If an unmarried teen mother does eventually marry, it is often many years later. And if she does not get married, she will experience the difficulties of single motherhood for many years.[4]

The teen mother is also much less likely to earn a high school diploma or attain college education by the time she is thirty. While many teen moms do eventually earn GEDs, many fewer complete even two years of college. Further, the gap—fewer high school diplomas or GEDs, less college education, and lower salaries—seems to be worsening. Teen mothers who were themselves born in the late 1950s had better outcomes than younger pregnant teens born in the early 1960s. If this is a continuing trend, the consequences for teen girls today could be much worse than what we describe here. Only time will tell.

Teen mothers themselves are not the only people suffering negative consequences. Being the child of a teen mother is also associated with negative outcomes. Teen mothers are more likely to give birth to a premature or low birth-weight baby,[5, 6] conditions that can be associated with infant death, blindness, deafness, respiratory problems, mental retardation, mental illness, cerebral palsy, dyslexia, and hyperactivity.[7]

> *The teen mother is much less likely to earn a high school diploma or attain college education by the time she is thirty.*

In addition, after taking into account many socioeconomic factors surrounding the teen mother, studies show that children of teen moms tend to have lower academic and cognitive outcomes in kindergarten. Later academic achievement also appears to be affected. A girl is less likely to complete high school if her mom was eighteen or nineteen at her birth compared with a girl whose mom was twenty or twenty-one years old. And this finding is likely to be a small reflection of a greater trend: We see improved academic outcomes for children whose mothers wait even longer—until their mid- or late twenties—to have them.[8]

Children of teen mothers are at greater risk of experiencing negative consequences in other parts of their lives, as well. After taking into account many socioeconomic and other demographic factors, study results indicate that mothers who are fifteen or younger at the time of their first birth are more than twice as likely as mothers who are twenty or twenty-one at the time of their first birth to be reported for child neglect or abuse. Further, mothers who are twenty-two or older at their first birth are less than half as likely as the twenty- to twenty-one-year-old mothers to be reported for abuse or neglect.

This association is also evident when we look at foster care. Children of mothers who were fifteen or younger at their first birth were 50 percent more likely to have a child placed in foster care than women who were twenty- to twenty-one years old at the time of the first birth. Children of women who were twenty-two or older at first birth were significantly less likely than the children of twenty- to twenty-one-year-old women.[9] Therefore, the age of a mom affects not only her children's academic achievements, but also their well-being throughout childhood.

And the effects of a mother's age at the time of delivery of her child do not stop when the child is out of childhood. Aside from lower high school graduation rates, the daughters of teen mothers are much more likely to have their first children when they are also teenagers.[10] The boys of young mothers also experience negative consequences. When compared to the sons of mothers who were twenty or twenty-one years old when they had their first child, sons of mothers who were seventeen or younger were significantly more likely to be incarcerated and to remain incarcerated for longer periods. Sons of mothers who had their first child at twenty-two or older were significantly less likely to experience time in jail or prison. So we see that delayed childbearing often has a positive effect on a child, and—as seen in this research—at least through his thirties and forties.[11]

The effects, in fact, are felt through generations. The direct cost of teen childbearing to society is estimated at about $28 billion annually— or roughly $84 for every man, woman, and child in the United States. And, as staggering as this number is, it does not take into account many other costs that are less easily measured: stolen goods, destroyed property, personal injuries, child welfare services (aside from foster care), as well as many other indirect costs to taxpayers and society.[12]

Yet not all teen pregnancies carry such high costs. For example, the social, financial, and academic outcomes among married teens may be much better than for unmarried teens.[13] Many young married couples are excited about the prospects of having a baby, even when the pregnancy was not strictly planned, and provide a stable two-parent home for their children. However, the proportion of births to married teens is small.

More than half a million women in their early twenties become single moms every year.

In 2008, more than 80 percent of births to eighteen- to nineteen-year-olds and more than 90 percent of births to fifteen- to seventeen-year-olds were nonmarital.[14] This represents a big change from the 1950s, when only about one in seven teen births was nonmarital.[15]

College-age women have also experienced an increase in nonmarital births, with more than 60 percent of births to women in their early twenties occurring out of wedlock in 2008.[16] The impact of this statistic is significant. There are about 1.7 million pregnancies among twenty- to twenty-four-year-old women every year, which lead to about 1 million births and about 400,000 abortions.[17] This means that more than half a million women in their early twenties become single moms every year, leaving many of the resulting children without fathers intimately involved in their lives. Also, remember that many of these single mothers have to interrupt their studies, delaying or perhaps scuttling forever the hopes they had for their lives.

Pregnancy and Contraception

Although many teens and young adults do not know all of this information, they have seen enough to know that teen and nonmarital pregnancy can block many of their goals and dreams. Some girls respond by waiting to have sex, but many others are sexually active. What are sexually active teens doing to prevent pregnancy?

A nationwide study of US teens, the National Survey of Family Growth, has shown that, since 1995, more than 95 percent of sexually active fifteen- to nineteen-year-olds have used some form of contraception at some point.[18] The most commonly used method in the most recent survey was the condom. Ninety-five percent of sexually experienced teen girls have used one. The next most popular contraception choices were withdrawal and birth control pills, with slightly more than half of girls reporting using each of these methods. When sexually active girls in this survey were asked if they used any contraceptive the last time they had engaged in sex, about 30 percent said that they used the pill. A little more than half said that they had used a condom.[19] Less than 50 percent of sexually active teens maintain consistent condom use over a one-year period.[20]

Although more than 80 percent were using some form of contraceptive the last time they had engaged in sex, there is no measure of correct or consistent use. Further, while condoms offer the most risk reduction for sexually transmitted infections, they do not provide the level of contraception that the pill does. All of these factors contribute to a high risk of teen pregnancy among fifteen- to nineteen-year-old girls in the United States.

What about young women over the age of eighteen? How are they trying to prevent pregnancy? Of eighteen- to twenty-nine-year-old women who are in a sexual relationship and are *not* trying to get pregnant, a full 49 percent use a contraceptive method inconsistently or not at all.[21] One study, in which college men were asked about condom use over the last three months, found that 43 percent put on condoms after starting sex, and 15 percent took off condoms before finishing.[22] And so it appears that young adults are not any safer than teens.

How effective are most contraceptive methods? To find out, we need first to define effectiveness. It is measured by the pregnancies that occur over a year while using a certain form of contraception. In other words, how often does a given method fail? We can measure the failure rate under ideal conditions, or in the "real world." Ideal conditions are seen, for example, in studies by pharmaceutical companies, where study participants are careful to use the contraceptive exactly as directed. This is called "perfect use."

Then there is "typical use." According to a 2002 National Survey of Family Growth, the typical use failure rates in the US are about 17 percent for condoms and 9 percent for birth control pills. We see that the condom and birth control pill failure rates are greater for females under the age of thirty than for older females, probably because of inconsistent use by some teens and young adults.[23] When examining the number of pregnancies that occur over the course of a year when women use birth control pills for contraception, teen girls have an almost two and a half times greater failure rate, and young women in their twenties more than one and a half times that of women over age thirty.

When looking at condom failures, teens and young women under thirty have about one and a half times the failures that women over thirty have. Therefore, a typical sexually active teen girl or young woman who is using one of these forms of birth control will have a 10–20 percent chance of becoming pregnant within a year. In other words, between ten and twenty of every hundred girls or young women will become pregnant in a year. If a sexually active young woman is using fertility awareness (such as the calendar or rhythm method) or withdrawal as her contraceptive method, her risk of pregnancy is even higher.[24]

> Though contraceptives significantly reduce the risk, girls who use one of the common forms of birth control are left with a 10–20 percent risk of pregnancy.

A teen girl who was the daughter of a representative of one of the largest Christian ministries in the United States came to see Joe. She had become pregnant and was scared. Her parents were devastated. But they were kind, forgiving, and gracious. The daughter allowed her baby to be adopted. Unfortunately, she did not learn her lesson. These parents allowed the girl access to contraception, but she used it only sporadically. A year later, she returned to Joe's office, pregnant again. Finally, a year later, she returned one more time. She was pregnant again and once more adopted the child out. This entire experience was devastating to the parents and to the girl. All this had occurred before she was twenty. Although this girl's experience of repeated pregnancies is somewhat unusual, it is still common, as the statistics show, for a girl to be using contraception (sometimes correctly and sometimes not) and to become pregnant—and to be startled that she did.

> *Unplanned pregnancy among girls results in life-altering consequences, often associated with adverse social, economic, and health outcomes.*

Teen girls and college-age women who are sexually active are at great risk of becoming pregnant. Even though contraceptives significantly reduce the risk, girls who use one of the common forms of birth control are typically left with a 10–20 percent risk of pregnancy per year. And, because many of these girls will be sexually active for many years before they want children, they, and also their parents, need to understand that the risk of contraceptive failure adds up over time. The risks of contraceptive failure we have examined above are based on only one year of use. As time goes on, the percentage of failures will be even higher.

Then there are other issues. Long-acting birth control methods such as Depo-Provera, which are often used for teens, carry with them a lot of side effects. These include acne, bleeding, and weight gain. A young woman came to see Freda for prenatal care. After her baby was born, the girl had Implanon, a long-acting hormonal implant, placed in her arm. But when she experienced irregular bleeding, the girl had it removed. Two months later, she returned—with a positive pregnancy test. Now this young woman, who is still under age twenty, has two children.

Unplanned pregnancy among girls results in life-altering consequences, often associated with adverse social, economic, and health outcomes for the mother, father, and child. The far-reaching impact of teen and unplanned pregnancy makes it imperative that parents understand these risks and communicate them with their daughters. If you don't do it, who will?

CHAPTER SIX

Emotional Attachment

AFTER A FEW WEEKS, almost all parents (adoptive or biological) ask, "Is this child attaching to us?" Emotional attachment is one of the most marvelously striking characteristics of being human. It is not only a rich process; it is a necessary one for healthy emotional development. Attachment also appears necessary for healthy physical development.

Most of us have heard by now of the orphaned Romanian babies who failed to grow in a healthy way because they were not held and cuddled. They were deprived of attachment to other human beings.[1] Emotional attachment is vital to adults, too. For example, in one study, married women were subjected to a light and safe shock. If a woman's husband was holding her hand, she was able to tolerate the shock much better. Women found the shock less unpleasant if holding their husband's hand, rather than the hand of a stranger, or no hand at all.[2]

Researchers at Ohio State University report that relationship intimacy is positively associated with better health, including strengthened immune systems and shortened healing times for physical wounds. In contrast, they say that high-conflict marital relationships are associated with weaker immune systems and a higher likelihood of disease, especially among women, as well as a lengthened healing time for wounds.[3]

This characteristic of human nature, the absolute requirement for attachment to other human beings to ensure the best chance for emotional and physical health, seems to be present even before birth. We are discovering a "biochemistry of connection."[4] As Allan N. Schore of the

> *Attachment is a significant and good aspect of the way we are made.*

UCLA School of Medicine describes it: "The idea is that we are born to form attachments, that our brains are physically wired to develop in tandem with another's, through emotional communication, beginning before words are spoken."[5] Attachment is a significant and good aspect of the way we are made.

What do we mean by "biochemistry of connection"? Isn't the need or desire for connecting with another person just an emotion? Don't we simply feel connected if we want to and don't feel connected if we don't want to—sort of like deciding to listen to one CD instead of another? Not exactly! Our brains are the Grand Central Station of "connecting," which is a much more physical process than most of us would ever guess.

More physical? How can thoughts be physical? Here is a summary of what modern neuroscientists have shown us during the past few years about connecting.

First on the list is oxytocin, a hormone released by the pituitary, a small gland at the base of the brain. Of the hundreds of hormones present in the brain, some remain there and some, like oxytocin, spread to other parts of the body via the bloodstream. As a matter of fact, the brain is a cauldron of hormones guiding a lot of our thoughts and actions. These hormones play an enormous role in how we think, how we feel emotionally, and even in our decision making.

At any rate, oxytocin is released when a woman is in labor. It circulates via the blood to her uterus and helps make her contractions strong enough to push her baby out. But oxytocin doesn't stop there. It continues to be produced after delivery. It causes the mother's milk to be "let down" and continues to do so for as long as she nurses. But from birth on oxytocin plays yet another amazing role: It appears to help the mother "connect" or "bond" with her baby.[6] It has been shown that when the baby and mother are skin to skin immediately after birth, a large amount of oxytocin releases from the mother's pituitary. This seems to facilitate bonding to the baby.[7]

The bonding effect of oxytocin appears to be very powerful.[8] We all know that mothers will die for their babies. One of the most poignant examples is the woman found huddled over her child in Pompeii after ash from Mount Vesuvius covered the city and killed the inhabitants.[9] This kind of attachment or connectedness is often a very good thing. The connection a mother feels with the baby helps ensure that she will not just hear the baby's cry but will "feel" it—and respond to it. This is one reason a mother will greatly inconvenience herself to watch after her infant or child.

Then there are the amazing things in our brains called "mirror neurons." These cells, discovered by Italian neuroscientist Giacomo Rizzolatti, may be one of the most important survival mechanisms in children's bodies. Psychologist Daniel Goleman explains that "imitative learning has long been recognized as a major avenue of childhood development. But findings about mirror neurons explain how children can gain mastery simply from watching. As they watch, they are etching in their own brains a repertoire for emotion, for behavior, and for how the world works."[10]

A need for connectedness is wired into our brains when we are still in our mothers' wombs.

So we see that not only is it important for the mother to bond to the baby so she will be "driven" to care for and feed it. It is also necessary for the baby to bond to his or her mother and father (and others). This bonding with other human beings enables the baby to "learn" basically everything he or she must "do" to live. This dual process is critical from birth on throughout infancy, childhood, adolescence, and young adulthood.

A need for connectedness is wired into our brains when we are still in our mothers' wombs and seems to be passed on in our genes, from generation to generation. Daughters of affectionate mothers often become affectionate mothers themselves. Likewise, daughters of abusive mothers are often abusive to their own children. It appears that this is not just learned behavior, but that changes occur in the genetic material itself and can be passed on to subsequent generations.[11]

Now let's see how connectedness affects us in other ways. It is not just a play on words to say that sex and connectedness are integral to each other. As a matter of fact, sex *is* an intense experience in the mind—an experience of deep connection. We mentioned earlier that oxytocin is released when a baby and mother are skin to skin, and that oxytocin causes an intense emotional attachment. Interestingly, oxytocin does not only release into a woman's body when a baby is born. It also happens when she has close physical contact with a man, such as hugging, holding hands, massaging, or cuddling—and, of course, during sex.[12, 13] Research seems to show that oxytocin in these cases has the same impact on her brain function as it does with cuddling a baby—the affected girl bonds to the guy.[14]

With intercourse, oxytocin surges into a woman's body. If she has intimate contact and/or has sex with a male, a bond unconsciously develops. This connectedness is not just on an emotional level. It results from a real chemical acting on real brain cells, causing those brain cells to fire electrical impulses that result in thoughts, feelings, and actions that are different from those that would have occurred without oxytocin's impact.

We cannot overemphasize oxytocin's impact on human behavior. Oxytocin plays a major role in causing men and women to stay together for years on end. Just as nature has provided a built-in mechanism to ensure that infants are not abandoned, so it has provided a mechanism that helps keep sexually active couples together as well. A large percentage of married people in America stay together for many years.

Most of us do not realize that studies clearly show that it is rare for a woman or her husband to have sex with others while the marriage is intact.[15] The significance of this fact is obvious. Tightly connected, intimate couples are more likely to stay together. This greatly increases the likelihood that their children will be raised in nurturing two-parent homes, which provide the best environment for them to reach their full potential.[16]

Knowing this helps answer a common question. Why will a girl or woman stay with a guy who is abusing her? Part of the answer may be that oxytocin "binds" her to him, and she then finds it almost impossible emotionally to leave him. By the way, oxytocin has another effect on women. It can cause them to trust another person, perhaps more than they should.[17, 18] Louann Brizendine, a neuropsychiatrist at the University of California, San Francisco notes:

> From an experiment on hugging, we also know that oxytocin is naturally released in the brain after [a] twenty-second hug from a partner—sealing the bond between huggers and triggering the brain's trust circuits. So don't let a guy hug you unless you plan to trust him. Touching, gazing, positive emotional interaction, kissing, and sexual orgasm also release oxytocin in the female brain. Such contact may just help flip the switch on the brain's romantic love circuits.[19]

Sex, including the attachment it can produce, can be and often is hijacked from its original healthy purpose. As with almost any human characteristic, such as our need to eat, distortion of a healthy drive can cause real and sometimes life-altering problems. Sex can be healthy and fulfilling, or unhealthy and destructive.

The following findings of researchers who have studied human sexual behavior show how much we humans are secretly influenced by the chemicals, hormones, and electricity coursing in our brains. While we are not robots, we can find ourselves acting almost unconsciously. This kind of acting-without-thinking-about-it behavior can be both common and dangerous among adolescents and young adults. It allows brain activity to "control" them without their even knowing it.

We need to remember that the brain does not attain full maturity until we reach the mid-twenties.[20] The last portion to mature is the prefrontal cortex (the front of the brain behind the forehead). This area is the seat of cognitive thought: decision making, judgment, "seeing" what might happen in the future as the result of a decision made today, and moral reasoning.[21] The significance is that the brains of people younger than about twenty-five are less physically developed and therefore less mature than adult brains.

These yet-to-mature brains translate to adolescents being unable to make the most mature decisions about their behavior. This does not mean these young people are dumb. Many teens have high IQs and are able to do wonderful things—yet they can make terrible decisions. The issue is not whether they are smart or dumb. Their prefrontal cortexes simply are not fully developed. This factor, of course, isn't the sole cause of poor decisions. Lack of information, stress, rebellion, and more can also play a role. And young people are even more at risk if they lack the guidance of caring adults.

We need to understand that young brains are being molded all the time.[22] Actually, that's true for all of us, but the changing and molding happens much faster in young people's brains, and often with lifelong effects. Our brains mold in response to input from the world around us—in other words, from our experiences. When we have an experience, the very fact that we remember it means that some of our brain cells have connected with it. Our brain literally changes physically to allow that memory to be there. In the same way, when we develop a habit, it means some brain cells have regrouped, or re-formed.

So in reality, a habit is physically *in* the brain. This is similar to the habit a violin player has in fingering the strings. One study of the brains of violinists and people who don't play the violin showed that the portion of the brain that controls the fingers of the left hand (the hand that right-handed musicians use to finger the strings) is different in violinists than the same area of the brains of individuals who are not violinists.[23] Our brains change to support our activities and behaviors. In violinists, the brain develops a larger area to control the left hand so that the violin player can perform rapid and intricate movements with his or her fingers. This enlargement can be "seen" by modern neurologic studies.

The same process is at work in the brain as we develop self-discipline, our personal values, and on and on. These may seem to be "just there" as thoughts and feelings. Actually, our experiences mold our brains to produce these "habits of mind."[24] As we explained earlier, sexual activity produces an intense brain experience. Sex, which we think of as a purely physical activity, molds the brain—for good or for bad. It depends on the experience.

Freda saw a woman, aged thirty-eight, who came in for an office visit stating that she wanted to enjoy her husband of fourteen years as much as she enjoyed pleasuring herself. It seems that she had "accidentally discovered" herself while in the shower at age fourteen. For years she had used masturbation three to four times per week in order to "wait until marriage."

Now this woman, even though she desired her husband sexually, found herself having to self-stimulate after intercourse to "finish." It had not occurred to this well-intended wife that all those years of masturbation had developed a pattern in her brain that programmed her into pleasuring herself—and making it hard for her husband to compete.

Another hidden influence is estrogen. A girl's brain is bathed in her mother's estrogen while she is in the uterus. It is again bathed in the estrogen her own ovaries produce soon after she is born and for a number of months afterward.[25] Then, before puberty, a girl's ovaries again begin producing estrogen. Very soon, however, the estrogen levels fluctuate, allowing the menstrual cycle to happen. This fluctuation is necessary for ovulation and for preparation of the lining of the uterus to receive a fertilized egg and continue as a pregnancy. Estrogen has a huge impact on a girl, and so do the fluctuations, as the parent of any teenage girl can attest.

For the purpose of this short discussion, we will mention only one of the startling sexual effects of estrogen on a girl. Estrogen drives her craving for sexual intimacy. Estrogen levels are associated with lust and a desire for sex.[26] In one study, women with higher levels of estrogen were more likely to kiss, flirt, and have serious affairs. The women with higher levels of estrogen were also more likely to be considered attractive by men.[27] Estrogen also stimulates the activity of oxytocin in females.[28, 29] It seems that estrogen even helps produce an intense desire for bonding in females and makes women appear attractive to many men. This combustible combination can make a girl very vulnerable to a guy who might take advantage of her drive for intimacy.

Another significant player in our list of hormones is dopamine, which is called the "reward hormone." If we do something fun or exciting, dopamine makes us feel good. It makes us want to do it over and over. These dopamine-rewarded actions produce in us a sense of well-being.[30] Dopamine is a vitally important hormone. Without it, children would not have the courage to become independent of their parents. Venturing into the world is dangerous. Dopamine helps us overcome our normal fear—by making us excited when we try new and even dangerous things.

Dopamine is values-neutral, however. It can make a young person feel really good about making an A in school or catching a pass and winning a football game. But dopamine can also make people feel really good about taking drugs or having extramarital sex. And of course the good feeling makes the person want to repeat the activity, whatever it is.

The brain is dynamic. It is constantly being molded.

Next up are pheromones. Glands in the skin of many animals and of human males and females are the sources of this little-understood chemical. This chemical, however, is designed to go airborne. These hormones can have a powerful impact on the person who breathes them in.[31, 32] The strange thing, though, is that we are rarely conscious of them. Research shows that pheromones are involved in a woman's sexual attraction to a specific type of man. They also play a role in her sexual satisfaction with a man.[33, 34]

Of course the reason these chemicals can have such a powerful effect on us is because of our brains. The human brain is composed of approximately 20 billion neurons and 240 trillion connections (synapses).[35] It is, without question, "the most complicated three-pound mass of matter in the known universe."[36] But the brain is so much more than a "mass of matter." It is dynamic. It is constantly being molded. Molding is a lifelong process, faster in young age and slower in old age but continuing throughout life.[37] The connections (synapses) grow or deteriorate based on our thoughts and actions and our experiences.[38] If the brain were not moldable, we human beings would never be able to adapt to the outside world and survive.

We mentioned earlier how vitally important hormones are to the survival of human beings. These hormones are designed for the express benefit of humankind! Estrogen makes a woman desire sex, and pheromones attract her to her spouse. Oxytocin serves to connect a woman at a deep and abiding level with her spouse. Avoiding sex until settling down with one man "programs" the woman's brain to accept that as normal and desirable behavior. Oxytocin in a woman's brain bonds her to a baby so that she is driven to care for the child.

Next, the dopamine reward signal makes sex enjoyable and causes couples to desire the repetition of that act over and over. This, of course, facilitates pregnancy and birth. These decisions and behaviors strengthen marital bonds, which lead to long-lasting, intact families, which science has shown to be the environment most conducive to a child achieving his or her potential. Though these are very personal and significant life events, they are vital to the continuation of the race. It is an amazing system literally staggering in its beauty and complexity. These hormones form part of the reason why many, many marriages really can last for many, many years.

Unfortunately, these mechanisms sometimes work against an "uncovered" young person's best interest. A girl who is left without guidance and protection can get caught in the hookup world. Her brain can become molded to accept these experiences as normal, and then she becomes terribly damaged. Here are two common scenarios.

Scenario One

A girl emerging into her teen years yearns to be bonded to her parents and to her peers. Her greatest fear is being left out. Her healthy inborn and estrogen-enhanced desire for social bonding is doing its work.

She is receiving much of the guidance she needs from her parents. They are spending adequate and appropriate time with her. Bonding and attachment are going well.

The girl's mom and dad give her some very appropriate general guidance about morals and behavior. They are a little afraid of being too rigid about such guidance and are fearful about setting rules too tightly. They worry this would cause their daughter to stop listening to them. They love her intensely and cannot stand the thought of her having intercourse before she is married. The idea of her having sex with a guy while young and unmarried is abhorrent to them.

The girl is physically attractive and has an engaging personality. At the age of fifteen, she begins dating a vivacious guy who is a year older and who has had sex with one girl prior to this relationship. During their six months of dating, they have become more and more physical. Now the boy fondles her breasts under her sweater and occasionally reaches down her pants.

Next, he pressures her to have intercourse. The girl thinks about what her parents have said about not having sex until an undefined "later time." But there is something about him that:

- makes her feel attached to him and not want to be away from him (oxytocin and estrogen and the inborn desire to be connected);
- makes her trust him (oxytocin);
- makes him "smell" good (pheromones);
- makes her excited when he touches her breasts or ventures his hand into her pants (dopamine).

The boy tells her that if she loves him, she should have intercourse with him. The girl, however, doesn't really want to and has been saying no. She feels too young at fifteen. Her parents have suggested that sex is not the best thing, and she is afraid of getting pregnant or contracting an STI. However, he has "facts" addressing all of her concerns—"facts" she has heard from her sex-ed class, from friends, from television and movies—from everywhere.

As he is undressing her, the boy continues to press his case very gently and persuasively: "You are not too young. It is okay to have sex when you feel ready. If you aren't having sex by this age you must be too uptight, too naïve, or too religious."

When the girl answers that she is not on birth control pills, the boy says she can get the "morning after pill" from the pharmacy tomorrow without telling anyone.

When she mentions a friend who got pregnant even after taking the morning after pill, he replies that she could get an abortion quickly—but of course pregnancy will not happen.

When she expresses worry about sexual diseases, he says that he has a condom and is clean anyway. Then the boy lies and says he has never had sex before.[39] When the girl tells him that taking such a big step just bothers her, he reassures her there is nothing to worry about.

The girl is now stripped of all reasons to say no, even though she really still does not particularly want to engage in sex. She is left uncovered, naked before his arguments and naked before her own natural sexual interest.

So they have sex.

Scenario Two

A girl emerging into her teen years yearns to be bonded to her parents and to her peers. Her greatest fear is being left out. Her healthy inborn and estrogen-enhanced desire for social bonding is doing its work.

The girl is not receiving the guidance she needs from her parents. Because she is not adequately bonded to them, she will more intensely seek bonding outside the home.

In fact, the natural attention she devotes to her face and figure intensifies because getting attention from "friends" is vital. Her makeup, attractive hair, and emerging figure are attractive and make this needy, unconnected girl appear more mature than she really is.

Naturally, she draws attention from boys—actually, she is working hard to *get* that attention. When she receives any attention at all, unbeknownst to her, the dopamine (reward hormone) flows. This good feeling makes her want more of this attention.

The young woman is invited to an unsupervised party at which alcohol is flowing. The whole experience is exciting. In addition to the alcohol, dopamine is flowing into her brain, making her want more of the excitement, more of the feeling of belonging, and more of the attention of guys.

Sex happens, whether oral sex or intercourse—and, with it, the dopamine, causing the girl to desire its repetition (even if it hurts and is messy and not romantic at all). Also, oxytocin is coursing through her brain, causing her to experience feelings of connection and trust for the guys—even if they are only treating her as a sex object.

Just as the girl is immature, so is her bonding mechanism. Young teen couples almost never stay together. The younger such couples are when they initiate sexual involvement, the more likely they are to have multiple partners by the time they are in their twenties. The girl and the boys she is having sex with are no exception.

The girl's sexual merry-go-round continues. All this time, her brain is responding to these experiences by molding, accepting them as what sex is all about.

These and other scenarios show that the significant and vital experiences of bonding and trusting are being short-circuited for many young people. The brain molding that occurs for many during this vulnerable time seems to prove that such attenuated relationships are all we can expect from male-female relationships, and from sex itself. Remember the fourteen-year-old girl in chapter 1 who had had twelve partners in two years but thought this was okay because she only engaged in sex with her boyfriends? A survey published in *Seventeen* magazine indicated that about 40 percent of participating teen girls said they would consent to a hookup even though what they really wanted was a relationship.[40]

From this and other studies, young people, both girls and boys,[41] have an intuitive sense that casual sex is not healthy. Aside from the harm of STIs and nonmarital pregnancy we have already examined, to close this chapter we will discuss some of the emotional fallout.

It's possible you may never have heard or read much about some of these problems that result from teen and nonmarital sex. That is, in part, because science is just now beginning to reveal them. Yet these issues of emotional damage may be the biggest, most significant problems of all.

Sexually active teen girls are more likely to be depressed than their virgin friends. In a study that controlled other factors, researchers found that sexually active girls are three times as likely to report being depressed as virgins. The researchers made sure their results were not simply because the depression in the girls caused the sexual activity, as is often assumed. It turns out that girls who were sexually active at the time of one survey were *more likely* to be depressed at the time of the next survey. But virgins who were depressed at the time of the first survey were *not more likely* than other nondepressed girls to be sexually active at the time of the next survey. So it appears that sexual activity is indeed associated with depression.[42]

In a different study, sexually active boys were found to be twice as likely to be depressed as their friends who were virgins. Even more startling and sad was the finding that sexually active girls were three times as likely to have attempted suicide as their virgin counterparts. The sexually active boys, however, were eight times as likely to have attempted suicide as their virgin friends.[43, 44]

This last study concerned high school young people. What about college men and women? We see the same outcome from sexual involvement. The American College Health Association Survey of autumn 2008 showed that a huge number of college students are dealing with depression and thoughts of suicide. The College Survey showed that 26 percent of male students and 33 percent of female students felt so depressed during the previous year that it was sometimes hard for them to function. Additionally, 39 percent of male students and 51 percent of female students felt that "things were hopeless" at some time during the past year. And, sadly, between 5 percent and 10 percent of students had seriously considered suicide over the last year. Approximately 1.3 percent had actually attempted suicide.[45]

> The brain can't tell the difference between a broken bone and a broken heart. It hurts just the same.

Exactly why depression is so common among unmarried young people who have become sexually involved is unclear. Some specific situations are clearly associated with emotional pain and depression. One is breaking up. Studies clearly show that when a couple breaks up, the person who is left feels incredible emotional pain. Indeed, brain scans show that this is the same area that shows physical pain.[46, 47] In other words, the brain can't tell the difference between a broken bone and a broken heart. It hurts just the same.

This fact is predictable. Sexual involvement always results in some degree of bonding because of brain hormones. This connectedness is then wired into our brains and becomes a part of who we are. Breaking up means tearing a part of "me," and "I" feel it intensely. We may feel this as depression. It seems that connecting to another person is so vital to us that when an intense connection is broken (and we have seen that sex produces an intense, even if unconscious, connection), it almost feels as if something in us has died.

Now remember that adolescent girls who have initiated sexual activity between the ages of fifteen and nineteen will have, on average, more than seven sexual partners during their lives. In contrast, girls who maintain their virginity until age twenty-one will have, on average, only three sexual partners during their lives.[48] (You will also remember that the risk of getting an STI rises dramatically with the number of sexual partners.)

The bonding-breaking-bonding cycle seems to have an even more ominous effect. The ability of a person to go on then to bond in marriage seems to be affected. Several studies have shown an association between sex before marriage and a higher divorce rate when those individuals do marry.[49, 50, 51] This would suggest that a woman's ability to bond to her husband, once married, is weaker if she has had previous sexual involvement.

Yet remember that in our first chapter we emphasized the fact that young women generally desire marriage, and when they marry, they don't want to divorce. Unfortunately, few people will tell these young women that sexual involvement in high school or college can undermine the happy marriage they dream of as teenagers.

Researchers have found a negative correlation between premarital sexual involvement and satisfying marriages. A new study at Brigham Young University finds that "married couples who had delayed sex while they were dating were more likely to communicate, enjoy sex, and see their marriage as stable than those who had sex early on. They also were generally more satisfied with their marriages."[52]

Having an STI can be another obvious reason for the rampant depression among sexually involved young people. Such an infection often causes feelings of depression, guilt, and shame.[53, 54] Joe will never forget the woman who was infected by her boyfriend with human papillomavirus and then developed genital warts. Unfortunately, the warts were extremely resistant to treatment, and it took four years to clear her up. She became depressed, anxious, angry, and confused—which were legitimate emotions. It was an emotionally devastating problem.

Even worse is the depression and sadness of women treated for infertility caused by sexual involvement in high school and college. Then there is the depression in women who divorce because they and their husbands just could not "work things out." Who knows whether this relational distance occurred because of a damaged ability to bond because of prior sexual affairs. Who knows how much angst, depression, and bitterness these women could have bypassed by avoiding sexual involvement until settling down with one partner for life (rarely accomplished in America except in marriage).

We have described some of the hidden mechanisms in the brain that either deepen our joy and sense of connectedness as relational beings or, when misused, can set us up for a lifetime of pain and failure. The dopamine that helps us take healthy risks can make us hooked on sex. The oxytocin that encourages healthy and necessary bonding can influence a girl to trust a guy who in a few years she would not even consider as dating material. And yet she may not only have sex with him once but continue the relationship for a long time.

We have already seen that STIs and pregnancy can permanently change a girl's life. They can end her chance of experiencing a pregnancy in her own body. In the case of an out-of-wedlock pregnancy, the baby who results may never be able to go to college (even though, intellectually, she is perfectly capable of attending one) because so many single teen girls who become mothers are in poverty for so long.

As we pointed out earlier,[55] this is all very heartbreaking. Many of the young women who say they want a career or graduate school will never get there. Many girls and young women are trapped into a relationship because of bonding they never expected. They are so depressed that they cannot study. Because they cannot achieve good enough grades or do well on the entrance exams, they never go into law school or medical school or have the chance to achieve whatever academic dreams they had. Their dreams are dashed. And yet they never knew the risk they were taking when hooking up back in high school or in their heady days as a freshman college student.[56]

Sexually active teen girls are five times more likely to be victimized by dating violence than girls who have never had sex. They experience lowered self-esteem and an increase in anxiety. As we have explained, even if no STIs occur and pregnancy does not happen, teen sexual activity has many negative consequences.[57]

If we stand back and consider all this information from a slightly different perspective, an amazing pattern emerges, one we perhaps may not have noticed earlier. Pheromones attract a woman to a particular man. Future research may even show that they can even attract a man to a particular woman. Estrogen in a woman's body can make her interested in sex and can make her more attractive sexually to a man. As a couple becomes physically involved and intimate as a result of this attraction and sexual interest, oxytocin can bind them together emotionally. As they engage in physical contact and sexual intercourse the dopamine makes sexual involvement a habit—a very enjoyable habit they want to repeat again and again. In most cases, this results in pregnancy and childbirth. The emotional attachment and resulting stable long-term relationship helps ensure that the children who arrive will be raised in a home with two biologic parents (or if children are adopted, in a home with two parents commited long-term). A home of this type has been shown by multiple research studies to provide the best possible environment to help a child achieve her potential.

The entire system of hormones involved in the sexual and relational aspects of human behavior seem designed to facilitate this stability of home environment and optimal environment for children to grow in. There has been great skepticism about marriage because divorce is so common. Yet the truth is that a majority of married people remain faithful, according to the largest and most reliable study ever done in America about American sexual practices, the National Health and Social Life Survey. When asked about fidelity in marriage, "more than 80 percent of women and 65 to 85 percent of men of every age report that they had no partners other than their spouse while they were married. These findings are confirmed by data from the General Social Survey, which reported virtually identical figures for extramarital sex."[58] The scientists from the University of Chicago who conducted the survey go on to say, "The marriage effect is so dramatic that it swamps all other aspects of our data. When we report that 80 percent of adult Americans age eighteen to fifty-nine had zero or one sexual partner in the past year, the figure might sound ludicrous to some young people who know that they and their friends have more than one partner in a year. But the figure really reflects that most Americans in that broad age range are married and are faithful."[59]

Clearly, research shows that these hormones work for men and women for the purpose of bringing them together and encouraging their sexual commitment and contact and helping to preserve the home for the resulting children.

So what future do you want for your daughter? Will you take seriously the pitfalls she faces? Will you provide the appropriate guidelines and limits, even when she fights them? Will you spend the time it takes to bond with her—even when it seems she doesn't want you? Will you provide "cover" for her? Will you refuse to leave her naked before the predatory pursuits of guys who have learned through long experience to manipulate a girl into bed? Will you cover her against her own immature but developing nature, a nature built into her that, when mature, will lead her to good relationships that are the "stuff of life"?

The decision is yours. Not all girls will follow this kind of guidance. But you will give yours an enormously greater chance of becoming the person you dreamed she could be when she was that miraculous baby you wonderingly held in your arms.

CHAPTER SEVEN

How Society Misleads Girls

AFTER READING THE FIRST SIX chapters of this book, you now have a deeper understanding of the sexual behavior of young people, the prevalence of STIs, the difficulties associated with teen pregnancy and teen childbearing, and the hidden world of brain development and emotional attachment. We never fail to be surprised and dismayed at the obstacle course of dangers facing our daughters.

We believe that it is inexcusable to ask a teen to make a responsible and informed decision about sexual activity when she does not have access to all of the information necessary to weigh the risks and the benefits. Of course, having it does not guarantee a responsible decision, but *not* having it makes a responsible decision much more difficult.

Unfortunately, our daughters face other obstacles. These obstacles involve not just a lack of good information, but actual *bad* information that can lead them down the wrong path. Because the research contradicting these untruths is so clear, we have chosen to call them lies, because a lie is an untruth purposefully told. We will examine some of these lies, showing that they contradict what research shows to be in the best interests of girls and young women.

Lie #1: Boys and Girls Are the Same

The first lie is that boys and girls are, despite the labels and expectations placed on them by traditional society, basically the same. This untruth allows many other lies to follow in its wake. Because "sex is sexist," generally burdening females more than males (e.g., pregnancy, cancer, infertility), it is important to realize that males and females are actually different in many respects.

> Men and women are both human beings, *but they are not the* same, *nor would we want them to be.*

But before we go any farther, we need to make clear that we are not saying that females are in any way *inferior* to males. *Different* does not mean *inferior*. For example, an orange differs from an apple, but no one would claim that an orange is *inferior* to an apple. They are both *fruits*, but they are clearly different. In the same way, men and women are clearly both *human beings*, but they are not the *same*, nor would we want them to be. Just as we can appreciate and enjoy the differences between oranges and apples, so we can appreciate and enjoy the differences between men and women. So let us go ahead and look at some of these differences.

Most obviously, there are structural differences between the sexes. Boys and girls are born with different anatomical features. Their bodies develop along different trajectories, with boys eventually reaching a greater weight and height, on average, than girls. Puberty occurs earlier for girls, on average, than for boys. These differences are all easy to see as young people develop.

Differences in brain development, on the other hand, are more difficult to gauge. With MRI studies, though, we now know that several parts of the brain develop more rapidly in girls than in boys.[1] We also now know that some parts of the brain, when fully developed, are larger in women than in men and vice versa, probably due to the difference in estrogen and testosterone levels in their brains.[2]

It also appears that gender-specific effects on brain structure occur when children are abused or neglected. For example, boys who were neglected at an early age have a small but significant change in their brain structure compared to boys who were not neglected, although boys who were sexually abused did not exhibit the same change. However, girls' brains show the opposite response. Girls who experienced early neglect did *not* have the same change in brain structure, but girls who experienced early sexual abuse *did* appear to exhibit the change.[3] While this information may appear somewhat confusing, it shows that male and female brains handle information and experience differently.

These are just three gender-related differences in brain structure and development we have elected to point out. With new studies being performed and published every month, it is quite certain that these findings are only the beginning of what we will soon know about the brains of boys and girls—information that will help us understand our children even better.

As you might expect, the differences in the bodies and brains of boys and girls translate into physical and emotional differences throughout life. This is especially true when it comes to sex. It has often been said that "guys give love for sex and girls give sex for love." Although several studies have shown that this is not necessarily the case,[4,5] guys and girls seem to desire sex differently.[6]

For example, when college men are asked for their "ideal" number of sexual partners, they will, on average, desire more than women will.[7] This difference has been measured in the US and indeed around the world, meaning it is not a mere cultural difference.[8] On average men desire more sexual partners, both in the short term and over the course of their lives.[9] Of course, this does not mean that men are incapable of being monogamous, or that monogamy goes against their nature. Nor does it mean that men will find that having multiple partners is ultimately more fulfilling. As a matter of fact, the number of short-term sexual partners they desire drastically falls once men are married.[10] But these studies do seem to indicate a difference in how young men and women envision the ideal sex life.

In a large-scale survey, men overwhelmingly said they engaged in sex for the first time because they were curious or "ready" for sex. Women, however, overwhelmingly answered that they did it out of affection for their partners.[11] This dissimilarity highlights another difference among men and women: Women are much more likely than men to participate in compliant sex when one partner desires sex and the other does not. Women frequently say they want to fulfill their partner's needs and prevent him from breaking off the relationship.[12] Further, young women are about four times as likely as young men to participate repeatedly in disliked sexual activities.[13]

A beautiful twenty-one-year-old woman came to Joe for an annual exam. She explained that she was "trying to learn to engage in anal sex" even though it was causing significant pain and discomfort. Why? It was what her boyfriend wanted.

Another time, a freshman university student came to Joe after the annual Texas-Oklahoma football weekend. She was feeling faint and experiencing moderate vaginal bleeding. Joe discovered a large tear in her upper vagina and asked what had happened. The night before the game, she had traveled with a guy to a hotel room in Dallas. She was a virgin when they walked in that night but not when she walked out the next morning. Because her hymen was so thick, the guy could not penetrate her, even after many tries. Finally, he grabbed her by the waist and jammed her down on himself, tearing through her hymen and upper vagina. The physical and emotional trauma this young woman experienced is hard to describe. But she engaged in sex because that is what the young man wanted.

Here is another difference: Males and females have different responses once sexual activity has taken place. Teen girls feel more regret for not having waited longer.[14] In the context of hooking up, college women are more likely to expect that the hookup is the beginning of a romantic relationship[15] and to feel regret and shame as a result of a hookup.[16] In one study, women who expressed regret over a hookup communicated feelings of shame and self-blame. The men who expressed regret, meanwhile, usually did so because they felt that they had made a poor choice in partner.[17]

A girl's expectation to be just like a boy is not borne out in her day-to-day reality.

The effects of sexual activity among teens and young women, however, can extend beyond mere regret, as we discussed earlier. One analysis of the Add Health study shows that teens who become sexually active are more likely than their nonsexually active peers to become depressed over the next year—especially girls. They are three times as likely as their virgin peers to become depressed.[18] Another study shows that young college women with the highest number of casual sex partners over the past year are the most likely to display depressive symptoms. This is not the case for young men.[19] Although research does show that boys may experience depression associated with sexual activity, it appears to be less than that experienced by girls.[20, 21]

Clearly, differences exist between males and females when it comes to sex. Knowing the differences allows parents to better guide their daughters through early relationships and feelings of romance. By blurring the lines of the differences and refusing to acknowledge their existence, society places girls at a real disadvantage. A girl's expectation to be just like a boy is not borne out in her day-to-day reality.

Indeed, a bestselling book entitled *The Hookup Handbook: A Single Girl's Guide to Living It Up* unwittingly acknowledges the differences between females and males. In Part I it outlines a "hookup contract" that each girl should make with herself. The contract purports to help prevent "hookup-induced drama and trauma." At least half of the contract points are intended to keep girls from forming—or at least revealing—an emotional attachment with the guy, and thereby limiting regret and "drama."[22]

Why would authors who dub their book a "guide to living it up" and who finish the book with the statement, "Your mother never had this much fun!"[23] spend so much time instructing girls to refrain from waiting for a phone call from their most recent hookup partner or imagining that their hookup may evolve into a stable relationship? We suspect it is because these responses occur frequently among young women, providing an outward display of the true feelings of many girls and of some of the inherent differences between males and females.

Lie #2: The Supergirl Phenomenon

Another way that society misleads girls is with strong messages of unrealistic expectations. *The Supergirl Dilemma*, a report by Girls, Inc., outlines findings from a survey of more than 2,000 school-aged girls. The report begins with the first finding, "The Supergirl Phenomenon": "Girls today experience intense pressure, at ever younger ages, to be everything to everyone all of the time." One ninth-grade girl says, "Girls are very pressured today to get good grades, look good, have a lot of friends, do a majority of the chores, and still have time for family." Elementary school girls had very similar responses on their survey, reflecting the pervasiveness of the message.[24]

> *Young women often feel they have to be smart, fun, pretty, sexy, athletic, accomplished, and sensitive to the needs of others.*

Society sends messages to our youth regarding what they should accomplish, when they should accomplish it, and what a "good" or "healthy" life is. Young women often feel they have to be smart, fun, pretty, sexy,[25] athletic, and accomplished—outperforming their male counterparts—and being sensitive to the needs of others as well. In addition, they should be able to will themselves into being "just like guys," without emotions that would hinder their sexual expression and emotional freedom. And, the culture says, they should desire and expect social and sexual satisfaction without any negative consequences.

One of the most popular young women's magazines, *Cosmopolitan*, had the following headlines on its July 2010 cover: "8 Foods That Keep You Slim All Summer," "The Sexy Secret to Making Smart Decisions," and "What Men Find Hot."[26] Clearly, girls and young women see these themes every time they go past the magazine rack at the local bookstore or supermarket.

Considering the results of the Monitoring the Future survey[27] (see chapter 1), it is clear that many girls have internalized this message and are acting on it. In that survey, high school girls reported that they work very hard at school and aim for very high academic and career achievements. To set themselves apart from other students, they have to achieve even more than their peers. How can they do that? One natural response is to limit the number of relationships they choose to develop.

In *The Hookup Handbook*, the authors recognize this as one of the factors driving the increasing prevalence of hooking up. They call it the "too-busy-to-have-a-boyfriend syndrome." The time it takes to nurture a relationship makes having one seem unattractive. The second factor is "defensive nondating," which is related to the first. If relationships are unpredictable and may lead to heartbreak, they become more of a risk to college life than a benefit. So, according to this book, the answer to these life problems is the hookup, where sexual satisfaction is met without the need for time or emotional investment.[28] So young women are putting off relationships until they have graduated from college or grad school, or until they have a well-paying job. In lieu of relationships, they are having hookups.

Where does hooking up leave young women? One study shows that hookups sometimes actually do result in them feeling "desirable," which is what many of them are seeking. However, just as frequently they feel awkward and confused.[29] Further, as we have seen, they can be left with pregnancy, sexually transmitted infections, and depression, any of which can change their lives permanently.

The pressure to be "everything to everyone" also encourages young women to partake in other destructive behaviors, especially alcohol abuse. Through media messages and campus culture, girls hear that the path to sex and fun is through alcohol. College women frequently overestimate the amount of alcohol that males want their female friends, dates, or sexual partners to drink. And those who hold this misperception actually consume more alcohol.[30] This study makes clear that societal messages can, and do, increase risky behavior.

Excessive drinking is common among active participants in the hookup culture. Indeed, alcohol appears to be a prerequisite. Beyond being part of the normal routine of hooking up, excessive alcohol drinking probably makes the entire hookup system function. Everyone seems to agree—from participants to those who are merely observing it—that alcohol is the ingredient that makes hooking up a growing and sustainable phenomenon.[31, 32, 33] Alcohol allows two people to overcome their natural anxieties and any sense of modesty or moral misgivings they might otherwise feel.

Lie #3: Cohabitation Is Smart

Societal messages also affect longer-term decisions regarding sex. One is that cohabitation is a preferable alternative to, or at least the most intelligent first step to, marriage. In one study, more than 60 percent of college girls "agree" or "mostly agree" that it is a good idea for couples to live together before they get married to make sure that they can get along in a domestic situation.[34]

Society keeps repeating the message to youth that cohabitation is normal and healthy, even smart—and that message is sinking in. Cohabitation is a growing trend. By 2002, more than half of all nineteen- to forty-four-year-old women in the US have cohabited at some point in their lives, an increase of *50 percent* since 1987. At the same time as the rise in cohabitation, there has been an almost equivalent fall in marriages. These trends are not limited to the United States.[35] These statistics, however, say nothing about whether cohabitation is a good thing.

Much research has been dedicated to this question, and the results may surprise many Americans. Despite its touted benefit of helping couples determine whether they are compatible, several studies have shown that cohabitation prior to engagement or marriage is associated with a higher rate of breakup.[36, 37, 38] Cohabiting before committing to marriage is also associated with lower marital satisfaction, dedication, and confidence, as well as increased negative communication.[39]

Studies also show that children living within a cohabiting relationship have worse outcomes. They are more likely to experience poverty, food scarcity, and housing difficulties.[40] These kids are also more than five times as likely to see their parents split up as children with married parents.[41] And childbearing for cohabiting partners is more likely, as cohabiting women have a higher contraceptive failure rate than either married or single women.[42] Further, cohabiting adults do not experience all of the health and financial benefits married adults experience, which include better physical and mental health and longer lives.[43]

Researchers point out some factors that could explain these different outcomes. The participants within a cohabiting relationship frequently have different goals for the relationship. Because a cohabiting relationship is usually not based on commonly agreed upon vows such as those seen in marriage (e.g., "'til death do us part . . ."), there is more room for individual interpretation of an appropriate end point for the relationship.

Also, men appear to value the freedom inherent in cohabiting relationships as opposed to marriage.[44] Considering that this "freedom" is in direct opposition to the stated goal of many girls to get and stay married for a lifetime, as well as the detrimental outcomes for the relationship and for any children, cohabitation is certainly a poor choice for young women.

Suppressing the Truth

So if marriage is such a clearly superior option, why do so many people choose to cohabit? If most parents and their daughters agree that academic success, job security, marriage, and children are worthy and important goals, then why are so few girls reaching them? What is blocking these young ladies from achieving their goals?

While the answer is undoubtedly multifaceted and complex, we simply must face the fact that the larger society is lying to our daughters—

> Mastering impulses and navigating adolescence and young adulthood is difficult. The challenge becomes even greater because of untrue messages from society.

saying that they need to look sexy, that sex is a natural and healthy part of adolescent relationships, that committed relationships need to be put off until after college, and that cohabitation is the wisest choice for a monogamous couple. Evidence presented thus far in this book demonstrates that plenty of girls are hearing and internalizing these messages, despite their destructive potential. When one considers all the pressures that girls and young women face today, it is not surprising that many are failing to reach their potential.

Mastering their own impulses and navigating through the social realm of adolescence and young adulthood is difficult even in the best of circumstances. The challenge becomes even greater when you factor in these untrue messages from society. Asking teens to make responsible decisions while denying them truthful, relevant information will, not surprisingly, lead to disappointing results for parents, girls, and, ultimately, all of society. We all lose when an entire generation grows up in a fictitious world where truth is suppressed and health sacrificed.

Now that we recognize the difficulties facing our daughters, how can we begin to change the social landscape to enable their success? This a book about hope, not despair. Over the next three chapters, we will discuss some approaches that can gradually change their world for the better.

CHAPTER EIGHT

What Is Society to Do?

WE HAVE JUST FINISHED outlining the messages that society delivers to our youth. Many of them are based on lies and lead our daughters down a destructive path. It's one thing, however, to describe a problem, another to offer a solution. So how should our society address these messages and provide our youth with an environment that contributes to their health and ultimate happiness? Better yet, what must we, as concerned members of this society, do in order to create a healthy environment in which girls (and boys) can reach their full potential?

To begin with, we must remember what we know. As discussed in chapter 6, the prefrontal cortex, which is responsible for calculating the risks and benefits of various choices and making choices accordingly, takes decades to mature into its adult form. This portion of the brain finally reaches this point only when people are well into their twenties.[1] How should this knowledge impact our society and guide parents? Several things come to mind.

First, society must recognize the important roles that parents fill in guiding their daughters through childhood, adolescence, and their young adult years. In recent years there has been an emphasis on the concept that "it takes a village" to raise a child, encouraging society to take an active interest in the care and education of its youth. However, there has not been an equal emphasis on encouraging *parents* to be active and authoritative in the lives of their youth. Here *authoritative* should not be confused with "authoritarian," which usually signifies tight control over someone else. Instead, *authoritative* suggests a warm and nurturing approach that also incorporates firm guidelines and expectations. Such *authoritative* parenting has been associated with the best outcomes for children.[2]

Second, society needs to combat the frequent media lie that parental guidance is uniformly bad, intended only to keep kids from getting what they want. Society needs to instead trumpet the truth that parents have the responsibility to care for their children until they become fully mature adults. Society has a stake in this process, as well. Society in general will be elevated by children who are guided well by parents. Therefore, society should support parents and encourage them to take an active role in the lives of their children, all the way through their young adult years. In part, this means engaging them in conversation and leading them toward critical thinking skills that will equip them for life in our complicated world.

> About half of all girls will contract an STI by the time they are twenty-five. That's not healthy.

Third, society also needs to stop repeating the lies that casual sex is good and even healthy. Sexual activity, as we have discussed, has many well-defined risks, as well as many more risks that are less clear. As we told you in earlier chapters, about half of all girls will contract a sexually transmitted infection by the time they are twenty-five.[3] That's not healthy.

As we have pointed out, these infections frequently display no symptoms but can lead to life-changing consequences, including infertility, chronic pain, and ectopic pregnancies. Further, two of these, HIV and genital herpes, are lifelong infections without a medical cure currently available. These sexually transmitted infections can affect a girl her whole life, and through her, her marriage partner, and her future children.

Besides STIs, pregnancy is a common and life-changing consequence of casual sex. Statistics say that three in ten girls will become pregnant by the time they are twenty.[4] This staggering finding places the prevalence of unplanned pregnancy among teen girls in stark relief and explains why many girls fail to reach their goals.

Sex is an unparalleled experience that, under the right conditions, can bind people into a strong and mutually beneficial relationship. But sex under the wrong conditions can also produce ugly consequences. In the case of teens and young adults, when their romantic relationships are temporary and all of their life plans are under construction, the risks of sexual activity significantly outweigh the benefits. In such circumstances, we cannot, in good conscience, recommend sexual activity to young people, even those who believe they are in a stable relationship and believe they are in love.

But a lifelong, mutually monogamous relationship, such as marriage, minimizes these risks and allows the full benefits of sex to be realized. If both partners have waited until marriage to have sex, the risk of STIs is virtually nonexistent. The risk of nonmarital pregnancy vanishes. And although unplanned pregnancy can still occur and complicate academic and professional goals, the presence of two committed adults sets the stage for a partnership in which each can enable the other to reach his or her goals and simultaneously give the child a strong, two-parent household.

> *We cannot, in good conscience, recommend sexual activity to young people, even those who believe they are in a stable relationship and believe they are in love.*

And, importantly, the two adults in this kind of relationship can experience freedom from the emotional and psychological burdens that weigh down those who have had multiple sexual partners before marriage. Isn't the contrast striking? Sex can look so different when you are experiencing it as an unmarried teenager rather than as a married adult.

Surely the gravity and risks of sexual activity during adolescence and prior to marriage outweigh its supposed benefits. This kind of sex is hardly a "healthy" choice for anyone's daughter (or son). By refuting this lie in the media and in our schools we help our daughters to reach their goals. If we do not speak up, however, we may well relegate them to a life of inferior accomplishments and limited fulfillment.

Fourth, we also need to expose the lie that cohabitation before marriage is a "healthy" or "intelligent" choice. Some voices present the freedom to choose cohabitation rather than marriage as an achievement of our modern society. They say it provides the stability and financial benefits of a marriage without all of the paperwork and other hassles. However, as we pointed out in the last chapter, recent research does not support this view. Cohabitation prior to a marriage commitment is almost never healthy or intelligent.

Cohabitation is linked to a greater chance of divorce when the partners *do* marry.[5, 6] It also is associated with a greater probability of contraceptive failure.[7] Children born within a cohabiting relationship are much more likely to witness the separation of their parents.[8] They are also more likely to experience poverty and food and housing shortages.[9] In contrast, marriage has been associated with many good health and financial outcomes that do not appear to pertain to cohabiting people.[10] So we should never consider cohabitation as a substitute for marriage, or even a good starting place for eventual marriage. Cohabitation may weaken any eventual marriage relationship, reduce the health and financial benefits that married people enjoy, and set the stage for worse outcomes in any children who might result.

Fifth, and more basically, we can help girls grow up in an environment that doesn't pressure them to meet a specific standard of physical beauty. This pressure, which comes at our girls nonstop from their peers and from popular media, often makes them feel hopeless and turns their focus away from relationship-building, academic achievement, and other age-appropriate endeavors.

We're not denying that physical beauty will always be important to every society. It encourages mating and, ultimately, the survival of the species. It is built into our brains to look for certain physical features in a potential mate.[11] However, we ought not to so narrowly define physical beauty as to make it simultaneously unattainable and the center of every girl's world.

Unfortunately, pop culture has set a physical standard of beauty that relies on overly thin models whose bodies are surgically "enhanced" and whose photos are airbrushed. These images, of course, cannot be achieved in the real world, but they have real-world consequences. The photos of impossibly thin girls are everywhere, and boys seem as aware of them as girls are.

As we saw earlier, girls feel this pressure to be thin, pretty, and sexually attractive to males starting in elementary school (if not younger!).[12] Where are they getting this message? It is, unfortunately, all around us.

The annual Teen Choice Awards show relies on teens to choose their favorite artists in television, music, and movies. Their most recent choices are telling. In the music category, Best Female Artist went to Lady Gaga.[13] In the TV category, Best Comedy went to *Glee*, Best Drama to *Gossip Girl*, and Best Reality Show to *Keeping Up with the Kardashians*.[14] Let us give you a quick rundown about why these choices are worrisome:

- Lady Gaga is best known for her pop music and outrageous fashion. Her chart-topping hit in 2009, "LoveGame," features the following lyrics (repeated many times): "Let's have some fun this beat is sick/ I want to take a ride on your disco stick." The music video shows a very thin Lady Gaga simulating sexual activity in her dancing with little to no clothing.[15]

- *Glee* is a primetime comedy about a motley crew of high school students who join a glee club at a Midwestern high school. The show incorporates many relationship and sexual issues. In one episode, several of the characters have music video fantasies about being Britney Spears. During these scenes, the female actors are dressed in revealing clothes and incorporate sexual moves (including simulated masturbation) into the music sequences. Soon after this episode aired, two of the twentysomething actresses took part in a controversial photo shoot for the November 2010 issue of *GQ*, dressing in lingerie and schoolgirl clothes while posing in sexual situations. The article title and tease copy were called "*Glee* Gone Wild: How Did a Show About Geeks, Gays, and Giddy Show Tunes Become the Most Popular Show on TV?"[16]

- The *Gossip Girl* drama follows a fictional group of wealthy and influential teens on Manhattan's Upper East Side. An anonymous "Gossip Girl" narrates, blogging about relationships, fashion, and pervasive sexual activity (often resulting in more than one sexual relationship per character per episode).

- The *Keeping Up with the Kardashians* reality show follows a blended family. Much of the focus is on socialite Kim Kardashian and her sisters, Kourtney and Khloe, who are all in their late twenties to early thirties and together own a fashion boutique. Like *Gossip Girl*, the show focuses on fashion, sex, and conflict-ridden relationships. However, because the stars of the show are older, the themes are consistently more mature than material typically intended for adolescent audiences.

If these are the most popular television shows and music artists according to teens, and the average eight- to eighteen-year-old spends seven and a half hours per day taking in media,[17] then teens are receiving a consistent, albeit misguided, message that the good life is full of sexual activity, dysfunctional relationships, and expensive clothes. This type of programming merely reinforces the lie that girls have little worth outside of their physical appearance, which will be measured against an unattainable standard. And if a girl cannot meet society's definition of beauty, then she may well feel the need at least to appear "sexy" to get male attention.

The American Psychological Association convened a special task force to address what it calls the "sexualization of girls." It defines sexualization as occurring when (1) people's value is derived solely from their sex appeal and sexy behavior; (2) people are considered sexy when they meet a narrow definition of physical attraction; (3) people are displayed merely as objects for sexual use without any characteristics of independent thought or action; or (4) sexuality is imposed upon people.[18] As our examples show, the mass media collectively are one of the strongest forces for the sexualization of our girls.

Recent photos of Suri Cruise, the daughter of Tom Cruise and Katie Holmes, walking in heels at the age of three have been widely publicized.[19] Her appearance apparently prompted an increase in the number of very young girls wearing dressy shoes with heels (and one- to two-inch heels are now available for kids about three years old and up).[20] Meanwhile, the Bratz® dolls wear high heels and heavy makeup, are said to be "flirty," and have the motto "The girls with a passion for fashion!"[21] Young girls today are surrounded by products that communicate the importance of leaving behind the things of youth and adopting an older and sexier look.

What can society do to change this unhealthy trend? Certainly we can stop consuming the products and programming that are giving our girls a distorted view of themselves and their place in the world. We have a choice about the products and programming we support, and we really can have an impact. Responding to a grassroots letter-writing campaign, for example, Hasbro canceled its sexually charged Pussycat line of dolls.[22]

Parents and schools can also encourage girls to develop media literacy. When children learn how to critically evaluate media messages, they can better judge media intentions and protect themselves from ill effects. Media literacy among young people lessens the internalization of a media-promoted beauty standard or ideal, just as it has effectively addressed media portrayals of alcohol use and violence.[23]

To combat the media's unrealistic physical ideals, we should also emphasize body competence and function above physical attractiveness.[24] By encouraging athletics and focusing on optimization of the body's abilities, we will be telling a girl that her body is not merely an object to be gazed upon, appraised, and used by guys. Rather, it is an integral part of how she functions as a whole person.

Sixth, society can encourage girls to continue practicing their religion or faith through their teen and young adult years. Many girls receive the message that their beliefs and religious practices are "juvenile" or "old-fashioned." Adolescents frequently may have heard that the university does not encourage religion. Indeed, students with traditional religious beliefs or practices sometimes *do* face scoffing on campus. This, however, is in the face of much research that demonstrates how beneficial religion and spirituality are to adolescents.

Teens who report themselves as spiritual or actively practicing religion are much less likely to participate in risky behaviors. They are less likely to participate in voluntary sexual behavior, drug and alcohol use, and violence.[25, 26] These teens are also less likely to commit suicide.[27] Further, it appears that just being involved in a community of faith lowers the chances that teens will be involved in risky behavior. Clearly, exercising spirituality and actively participating in religion reduce risky behavior and are healthy behaviors for youth.

If we want healthier young people, society should encourage religion and spirituality.

Sociologists are discovering that students who are religiously involved, and especially those who are deeply devoted to a relationship with "the Divine," are less likely to be depressed, more likely to avoid risky behavior, and more likely to show respect for themselves and others.[28] Laura Sessions Stepp, in her book *Unhooked: How Young Women Pursue Sex, Delay Love and Lose, at Both*, discusses this study, adding, "This leaves one wondering whether after all the ambitious child rearing that parents of this generation of students have done—all the Discovery toys, Suzuki piano lessons, four a.m. swim practices, SAT practice classes and summer camps in faraway places—they might have done as well or better and saved a lot of money by just taking their kids to church, temple or mosque."[29] Wise words!

If we want healthier young people, society should encourage religion and spirituality. This is especially true during the transition from high school to college, when teens are particularly apt to join in risky behavior. So college administrators, professors, and residence hall staff should create an atmosphere in which religion and spirituality are celebrated and encouraged.

How likely such help at the university level might be, however, is an open question. In the past, universities took upon themselves the responsibility of acting *in loco parentis*, functioning "in the place of parents."

Perhaps you remember your university fulfilling this function when you were in college. Unfortunately, this is no longer the case, and assuming that it is can be a fatal mistake—literally. Many parents have learned this to their horror after receiving a call from the university about a child who has died from an alcohol overdose or suicide.

Concerning sexual matters, many colleges and universities have moved from providing dormitories for men and dormitories for women to providing only mixed-sex dorms—and many parents and students actually agree with this change. According to one female student posting on the popular Suite101.com website, such living situations can be helpful because the world isn't separated into same-sex spheres: "Men and women need to learn to relate to each other, especially in the workplace, and a dorm can be good practice."[30] (To her credit, this author admits: "Sexual harassment can be a big problem in coed dorms. College girls can find themselves the victim of pranks and 'locker room talk' that crosses the line. Even if sexual harassment isn't going on, some college guys make girls uncomfortable with vulgarity and lewdness."[31])

These comments in favor of single-sex dorms remind us that college students do not yet have the cognitive ability of adults that would enable them to make the best decisions. Of course, just allowing young people to live in intimate proximity to people of the opposite sex shows an inexcusable lack of judgment on the part of adults who should know better. The abandonment of responsibility by both parents and universities to protect young women is nothing less than a dereliction of duty.

Universities, one of the most important social institutions of our day, are clearly not fulfilling their responsibilities. The Medical Institute surveyed a number of Texas universities about how they are providing sexual guidance and protection for their students. The results were dramatic. *Not one* had a coordinated or effective program for this purpose. Indeed, the dean of students at one university privately told our researcher, "We know the students do too much drugs, alcohol, and sex. We just hope to get them out of here alive."[32]

How our society chooses to educate, even mold, our boys will be critical in determining the ultimate destiny for our girls.

That kind of attitude is simply not good enough, and we can hold our schools to a higher standard—can, and must. Parents can refuse to allow their children to go to universities that will not provide proper guidance and protection for their children. Donors also must do some hard thinking. Is it reasonable to continue sending money to universities that apparently care so little for students that they provide them minimal protection—indeed, that actually insist students live in conditions that can damage them significantly?

What should we as a society expect if changes are not made soon? It would be fair to anticipate a significant decline in overall health, especially among girls. As we discussed in chapter 2, children who take in more sexual content from the media are more likely to participate in sexual activity at a younger age, get an STI, or have an unplanned pregnancy.[33] Research also shows a link between the sexualization of girls and an increase in eating disorders, low self-esteem, and depression.[34]

We have sought to reveal how the culture impacts our daughters. However, girls are only half of the equation. How our society chooses to educate, even mold, our boys will be critical in determining the ultimate destiny for our girls. And, currently, the contrast is striking.

Both boys and girls agree that parents send different messages about sex to their sons and daughters. More than half of girls report often hearing that attracting boys sexually is one of their most important tasks. And more than half of teen boys say that they often feel that they are expected to have sex.[35] In a large national survey, 78 percent of boys report feeling "way too much pressure from society to have sex."[36]

We need to tell boys plainly to be responsible members of society and make healthy decisions for themselves and for others. Further, we must *hold them responsible* for their share of the negative outcomes of casual sex, even when those consequences are only visible in the female partner—such as pregnancy and some long-term costs of STIs (including infertility). We ought to warn young men that they may be held financially responsible for any children they father until those children reach adulthood. They can and should expect the mother and the authorities to hound them for child support for years to come.

We all underestimate our potential influence. So few of us contact newspapers, television stations, companies, and politicians. But this is how things begin to change. We must insist that:

- drinking laws, especially for minors, be enforced;
- sexuality education programs in schools advocate abstinence and give accurate data about *both* the effectiveness *and* ineffectiveness of condoms and contraceptives; and
- the violence and graphic sex of media be put to a stop.

Parents need reinforcement from the larger society as they attempt to guide their children.

As we noted earlier, it has been said over and over that it takes a village to raise a child. This is only half right. It takes a village to *help parents* raise a child. We all need to pitch in and make sure the "village" does its job.

We also need to insist that marriage be honored by all public groups. As Shmuley Boteach says in his 1999 book *Kosher Sex*,

I know of almost no husband or wife who at one time or another has not sought or required the help and advice of family or friends who helped them pull through some difficult times. . . . Every community is responsible for offering newlywed couples the support and love they need to see themselves through the difficult times ahead, until this couple, too, will be ready to assist newlywed couples in their own time. It is for this reason that in the Jewish religion, a couple do not go on their honeymoon the morning after the marriage. Rather, for one full week after the wedding, a young bride and groom are entertained by their community to seven days and nights of festivities, thereby demonstrating the support, nurturing, and assistance of their entire community. The young couple are not castaways, all alone in their newly married life.

I remember when I first got engaged, and was plagued by all the usual doubts that accompany the big plunge into commitment and marriage, how an Australian rabbi whom I was friendly with saw me walking across the street in New York. With callous disregard for his own safety, he charged across the street, ran up to me, and gave me a big hug. "Congratulations," he said, "I just heard about your engagement. You are the luckiest man in the world. I worked with your fiancée when we were both teachers at a Jewish school in Sydney. She is the most amazing girl. I hope that my own children will one day find someone of such high caliber." He gave me another hug, and ran off. I remember thinking to myself, indeed, how lucky I was, which helped dispel the feelings of anxiety and melancholy that were gripping me at the moment. I also remember thinking what an amazing man he was, a truly righteous individual. One day when one of his children marry, I hope to be able to reciprocate this kindest of gestures.[37]

If we are serious about improving the lives of girls and young women, then we are responsible to help equip them to make decisions that will maximize their health and allow them to achieve personal fulfillment. Parents need reinforcement from the larger society as they attempt to guide their children. It is true that parents may still succeed in helping their daughters negotiate the complicated maze of the teen years even without society's help, but their job will be that much harder. It is in everyone's best interest—parents, daughters, sons, and the rest of society —to enable our daughters to achieve their potential and fulfill their dreams. And it starts with us, today.

CHAPTER NINE

What Are Parents to Do?

RELAX! **WHAT A REFRESHING WORD** in this mad world! But it is an important word, too—especially in raising a daughter (or a son). Recall that she is the daughter you conceived and brought into this world or (if adopted) chose to bring into your family out of love. She will most likely be your representative in the world long after you are gone.

Savor these years. Don't just endure them. Release your stress. Have fun when you are with her. Have fun when you think about her. Have fun when you talk about her. Your role is certainly serious, but don't take it so seriously that you destroy your enjoyment of this time—or perhaps hurt her. She is *your* child. Take great pleasure in this!

One of the inescapable realities of life is that this daughter of yours has been undergoing constant change, since even before she was born. She has been growing physically, mentally, and emotionally. The Greek philosopher Heraclitus must have said, "Nothing endures but change," in the midst of raising his *own* children! Our children's bodies obviously change, of course. But the relationship between parent and child must also change.

You know this intuitively: Our daughters *must* change in order to grow into independent human beings. They must become what you yourself are—someone who has set sail on the sea of life, launched by Mom and Dad. Just as a building requires a stable foundation to remain upright, so a child requires you to be a firm foundation as she grows into adulthood. Always remember that the foundation on which her life is built, the rock on which she stands in her growing-up years, the platform from which her ship embarks, is *you*!

The better your relationship with her, the more confident she will be in her foundation when the inevitable storms of life come. Research seems to indicate that spending time with her is critical to connecting with your daughter. But don't fool yourself about "quality" versus "quantity" time. *Both* are important. Remember, the Adolescent Health Study says that kids are less likely to be involved in a number of risky behaviors, including sex, if their parents are with them when they wake up, when they come home from school, during supper, and at bedtime.[1]

Then there is Frank Luntz's research (mentioned at the start of this book) that says how important it is for parents and their kids to have dinner at least five times a week. Kids who have dinner less often with their parents are more likely to be involved in many risky behaviors.[2]

The Search Institute, which has been studying what kids need in order to succeed for fifty years, lists forty developmental assets for children aged eight to twelve.[3] *The very first two of these forty* emphasize the importance of parental involvement:

- Family support—Family life provides high levels of love and support.
- Positive family connections—Parent(s) and child communicate positively. Child feels comfortable seeking advice and counsel from parent(s).

Spending time with your child does not mean you need to be "buddies." We are not talking about tolerating whatever she says or does. Foster Cline and Jim Fay's book *Parenting Teens with Love and Logic* notes that "*Love* does not mean hovering around your teens to protect them from all the rocks flung at them by the world. Nor does *love* mean tolerating outlandish, disrespectful, or illegal behavior. Rather, *love means maintaining a healthy relationship with our teens, empowering them to make their own decisions, to live with their own mistakes, and to grow through the consequences.*"[4]

It is important to talk to our girls, too—about anything and everything. As they get older, our conversations can and should cover big decisions, including sex. Multiple studies show that good communication correlates with less risk of a girl initiating sex at a young age. One study finds that children who communicate with their parents about sexual issues more than once feel closer to their parents and more able to communicate with them in general and about sex specifically.[5, 6]

Dr. Gary Chapman has written about fundamental ways people give and receive love (*The Five Love Languages*, a book mainly about marriage has sold more than four million copies worldwide). Dr. Chapman also applies the five "languages" for effectively expressing love to sons and daughters.

- *Words of Affirmation* communicate to a child how much you love her, express appreciation when she does something worthy of commendation, and encourage her when she is fearful.
- *Acts of Service* include anything you do for your daughter that you know she would like: mending a doll's dress, repairing a bicycle, etc.
- The giving and receiving of *Gifts* is a universal expression of love.
- *Quality Time* means giving your child your undivided attention—playing a game, reading a book, having a conversation. The important thing is that the child has your undivided attention.
- *Physical Touch* involves hugs and kisses, pats on the back, friendly wrestling on the floor. All of these communicate love.[7]

These ways of communicating love also help our children build up necessary self-esteem. Cline and Fay have some excellent suggestions:

Teens look to us for positive or negative affirmations, and they store them in their memory banks. The perceptions gained from these parental messages actually become their reality. Here are some tips on raising the odds for success as we exercise our responsibility to build the self-concept of our teens:

- Provide both stated and unstated messages that show you have unconditional love.
- Model your own healthy self-concept to your teens by taking care of yourself as much as you take care of them.
- Provide both stated and unstated messages that say, "I value you."
- Provide both stated and unstated messages that say, "You can think."
- Provide both stated and unstated messages that say, "You have control."
- Provide opportunities for teens to struggle through and own their decisions and responsibilities.

Three ways to show love are eye contact, touch, and smiles. In combination with each other, they're dynamite. The way we listen to teens also greatly affects how loved they feel and how much they love us.[8]

Why is self-esteem or, as Cline and Fay say, "self-concept," so important? First, it suggests that healthy connection or attachment between the girl and her parents has occurred.[9] Such attachment feeds a confidence into her that emerges as self-esteem. Poor self-esteem, conversely, could be a red flag to parents to evaluate their relationship with their daughter.

Next, healthy self-esteem in a girl probably reflects her understanding that she, including her body, is valuable and, as with anything of value, worth protecting. This includes using her body the way *she* wants to use it, not the way *someone else* might want to use it. Good self-esteem can give your daughter the self-confidence to make good decisions and to stay in control. It can help her smoothly transition through the years when she has acne, when other girls develop sooner or are considered more "popular." Positive self-esteem can give her the strength to withstand the constant sexualization of teen girls and other unhealthy social pressures.[10]

Finally, remember the power of mirror neurons that we mentioned in chapter 6 (discussing the brain and "attachment"). We said that imitative learning has long been recognized as a major avenue of childhood development. But findings about mirror neurons explain how children can gain mastery simply from watching. As young people *watch*, they are etching in their own brains a repertoire for emotion, for behavior, and for how the world works.

This is incredibly important. Our kids are not just learning from us as we *talk* to them. What they see us *doing* actually imprints on their brains, molding who they are from the time they are born and on through the teen years—and probably even afterward. They not only *learn* from us, they actually *absorb* us. What an opportunity and what a challenge for us, who must model healthy behaviors and mature decisions and avoid hypocrisy.

We have been speaking to parents in this chapter. Now let's get specific.

Dads are vital to the healthy development of girls. They contribute heavily to their daughters' sense of self-worth.[11] Cline and Fay weigh in on the importance of fathers' involvement with their daughters:

> Even though the girl is filling out, she still needs hugs from Dad and Mom. She still needs the touching, tickling, and roughhousing that the family has done in the past. The interpersonal relationships between daughter and parents should continue to develop as she develops physically.
>
> Regrettably, fathers sometimes feel nervous and quit touching their daughters. Girls may interpret this hesitancy as rejection, reacting in ways

their fathers don't know how to handle. A cycle ensues as the daughter's apprehension fuels her father's apprehension, and so on.[12]

Girls who experience good relationships with their fathers are more likely to have fewer boyfriends, more likely to postpone sexual involvement, and more likely to feel badly about having premarital sex.[13]

Jim Dobson, whose PhD is in child development, was on the faculty of the University of Southern California School of Medicine for fourteen years. He was also on the attending staff of Children's Hospital Los Angeles for seventeen years. In his book *Bringing Up Girls*, Dobson says:

> I want to say to all these dads emphatically that your pubescent and adolescent girls are going through a time of great insecurity. They desperately need you now. You are their protector and their source of stability. Your love now is critical to their ability to cope with the rejection, hurt, and fears that are coming at them from their peers. Hugs are needed now more than ever. I urge fathers to continue providing the physical contact that was appropriate during earlier childhood. It should not be sexual in nature, of course, but a loving, fatherly response is still vital. The last thing you want to convey now, even inadvertently, is that your love has melted away. So hide the awkwardness, Dad, and hug your kid like you did when she was six!"[14]

And, we might add, "Dad, if you don't, she may go looking for a guy who will."

Single parents have a particular challenge. But if you are single and have a child, you shouldn't feel alone or isolated. You are a part of a large tribe. More than half of US children will spend some time in a home with a single parent before they reach eighteen.[15] In 2010, 26 percent of children in the US were living in single-parent households, with 23 percent living with their mother only and 3 percent with their father only.[16] Of the recent adoptions from the foster care system in the US, about 31 percent were to single parents.[17] This is a huge change: In 1970, just 11 percent of children were being raised by a single parent.[18]

It is difficult enough for two people to solve the problems of parenting. The job of the single parent is even tougher. Not only is spending adequate time with your child more challenging, but the single parent often lacks someone who can give valuable feedback about subjects such as child guidance. Cline and Fay offer three cogent suggestions:

- First, make time for yourself, then make time for your kids.
- Second, don't speak negatively about the opposite sex.
- Third, separate what you can control from what you can't and then learn to live with both.[19]

Most single parents have heard that they need an adult of the opposite sex involved in the lives of their children, and this is generally a good idea. These adults can be good friends, relatives, and people from church or synagogue. They can even be grandparents. In fact, children often *want* to spend time with their grandparents anyway.

We have painted a very dark picture of the world in which teenagers and young adults live. How much influence can parents really have? Fortunately, in addition to data we have already presented in this volume, some encouraging scientific studies exist. Here is a sampling of a few of them:

- An analysis of the Add Health survey responses from about 12,000 teenagers found that those who feel close to their parents are less likely to engage in sexual activity.[20]

- In a separate analysis of Add Health surveys from approximately 10,000 adolescents in grades 7–11, those who perceive their mother's disapproval toward nonmarital sex are less likely than other adolescents to initiate sexual activity.[21]

- In a ten-year longitudinal study of 172 adolescents, a correlation has been noted between good communication (as perceived by the adolescent) with the parents (particularly the father) and the delay of sexual debut.[22]

- Reasons cited by adolescents for remaining abstinent: concern about pregnancy (94 percent), concern about sexually transmitted infections (92 percent), because of their parent's teaching (91 percent), and because of their own moral or religious beliefs (84 percent).[23]

- Adolescents who talk with their parents about initiating sex wait longer and tend to have fewer partners. An overwhelming majority (85 percent) of teens who talk to their parents about sex rely on parents rather than peers (9 percent) for information about sex.[24]

• Of adolescents who don't discuss sex with their parents, half (52 percent) still think parents are a reliable information source, while just under a third (27 percent) name peers as information sources.[25]

• Girls whose parents disapprove of their use of contraceptives have been found to be less likely to initiate sexual activity.[26]

Many parents may feel that their children do not want to hear from them about avoiding sexual involvement. Yet a number of studies indicate that many, if not most, young people intuitively know that sexual involvement is not in their best interests. Here are a few.

• Findings of the National Campaign to Prevent Teen Pregnancy reveal that 65 percent of teen girls and 57 percent of teen boys who had already been sexually active wish they had waited.[27]

• A survey done by the Kaiser Family Foundation and *Seventeen* Magazine reveals that more than nine in ten teens agree that being a virgin is a "good thing."[28]

• The National Campaign studies confirm that 90 percent of teens think it is important for high school teens to receive a strong message from society that they should abstain from sex, and more than 90 percent of adults agree.[29]

It is clear from all these studies that the responsibility for guiding young people about sexual behavior falls on the shoulders of parents. It is time for parents to get over the idea that they are powerless in this. Parents can no longer underestimate their importance in their child's eyes. One study, for example, showed that while 43 percent of adults think their teens' friends are most influential on matters of sex, only 18 percent of teens agree.[30]

And, when it comes to influencing their children, parents indeed have a number of advantages over peers, schools, churches, or even media. First, parents have been "connecting" with their girls since before birth. Parents have a unique relationship with their children that can

> *There seems to be less communication between parents and their daughters about sexual issues than there used to be. Don't let that happen.*

help in communicating difficult topics. Remember, parents are with their children year after year. No one else is—not teachers, not youth workers, no one. In one sense, this long-term relationship earns parents the right to communicate values to their children. Further, parents can take into account their adolescent's particular personality and sensitivities, as well as maturity—socially, emotionally, physically, and morally.

Unfortunately, there seems to be less communication between parents and their daughters about sexual issues than there used to be.[31] Don't let that happen in your home. It is *your* job to make it happen. Studies also show that discussions about sexual issues between parent and child often do not take place until *after* the child has already begun having sex.[32]

Before we talk about what to discuss with your daughter, we ought to briefly examine the environment in which these conversations take place. If your attitudes, words, and behavior support what you say, your words will be buttressed. If they conflict with your words, your children can be confused and your verbal message weakened. "If we want our teens to have self-control, we must model it," Cline and Fay note. "If we want our teens to be responsible, we must be responsible. If we want our teens to treat us and speak to us with respect, we must treat and speak to them with respect."[33]

Joe remembers one woman who came in for an annual exam. Divorced and now with a live-in boyfriend, she began talking about her fourteen-year-old daughter, whom she described as a very attractive girl. The mother was appropriately scared to death about the possibility of her teen engaging in sex, but she was totally blind to her hypocrisy. The fact is, studies show that adolescents whose mothers have cohabited are more likely than other adolescents to engage in early sexual activity and experience a teen birth.[34]

Family standards are very important. Young people often do not know what we expect of them about sex and sometimes feel that they are getting mixed messages. For example, if their mothers discuss birth control, they may think their mothers approve of their having sex. So it is important that parents be clear about their expectations. If they expect their child to be abstinent, they need to say this clearly.[35]

One of the clearest illustrations of family standards impacting young people's behavior—though an extreme one—occurred in Lakewood, California, in the early 1990s. Some popular high school boys gave each other "points" for every girl they could entice into sexual intercourse. Some were arrested for sexual assault. *Time* reported: "At the Belman home, where son Kristopher, eighteen, had returned after being released from custody, father Donaly said, 'Nothing my boy did was anything any red-blooded American boy wouldn't do at his age.'"[36]

The home environment can have a powerful influence. Here are some ideas that may help you communicate your values about sexual behavior:

- Provide information with sincerity, honesty, and good intentions. This provides the foundation for your message.[37]

- Monitor your child's life. Don't be excessively intrusive, but know what she is doing and with whom. This helps her avoid risky behavior.[38, 39, 40]

- Remember that essentially everyone is interested in sex. This certainly includes children, from the prepubescent years on up. Recall that estrogen causes interest in sex for girls. Testosterone does the same for boys. A child's interest in things sexual is good, normal, and necessary.

Be clear and specific in your guidance. The following are a few suggestions to tell your daughter, and you can add your own. We could have added a hundred more to this list.

- Remaining a virgin until marriage is realistic, and it is the standard of our home.
- STIs are a big deal.
- Pregnancy is a big deal—it will change your life forever.
- Condoms and contraceptives do not make sex safe.
- We do not approve of contraceptives for you until you are married.
- Others may not tell you the truth. Teachers, websites, and books may assert that you can have sex without worry. We will always tell you the truth.
- Males and females often have different attitudes about sex.
- Sex before marriage is sexist—it generally hurts the girl far more than it does the guy.
- The burden of setting the standards, therefore, falls on you. You must protect yourself to ensure your best chance of achieving your potential of health, hope, and happiness.
- We expect appropriate modesty.

- Parties with alcohol are off limits.
- Others will disappoint you, but they are not you; and no matter what they do, they do not determine what you do.
- Girlfriends will disappoint.
- Boys will disappoint.
- People in church or synagogue may sometimes disappoint.
- The majority of girls who have had sex say they wish they had waited until they were older.
- It is never too late to abstain.
- Sex has a much deeper meaning than its mere physical act.
- You will never be alone. You will always have me/us!

After all this comes the really hard part. You can't just dump this information on her and then move on. This message must be repeated—and repeated again. One study of teens and mothers showed that 73 percent of one group of mothers strongly agreed with the statement, "I have talked with my teen about sex," while only 46 percent of the teens strongly agreed that "my mother has talked to me about sex."[41] This shouldn't be a surprise. Authorities in parent-child communication emphasize the necessity of frequent repetition of your messages. They also emphasize, as we suggest above, that our messages contain valid information, delivered with clear expectations.[42]

Yet we often let fear of embarrassment keep us from saying what we ought. One survey found that more than 80 percent of parents agree with the statement: "When it comes to talking about sex, parents often don't know what to say, how to say it, or when to start." And teens wholeheartedly agree![43] But when teens are asked what would be the most effective way to reduce teen pregnancy, their most common answer is "more open conversations with parents."[44]

Another frequently cited reason parents do not talk to their children about sex is the desire not to be a hypocrite. Parents sometimes feel that if they have participated in sex outside of marriage, they cannot ask or expect their own child to refrain from sex until marriage. This is neither true nor wise. Your words still carry enormous weight. So be open and honest, appropriately, about your past. Your negative experiences can even serve as one of the strongest deterrents your child has for avoiding such involvement.

Years ago, a thirty-five-year-old mother brought her thirteen-year-old daughter in for the "Talk." This woman did not want her having sex until she was married. However, Freda knew that the mother was living with someone who was not her husband. So Freda asked what she thought about serving as a role model for the behavior she desired to see in her daughter. Faced squarely with this contradiction between her words and her deeds, the mother accepted the challenge, and her relationship ended. Five years later, the daughter left for college—as a virgin.

Joe has a dear friend whose daughter found some journal entries he had written about his past sexual involvement. The daughter asked her father about his earlier sexual involvement. The ensuing discussion and resulting transparency opened up family members to each other in healthy ways, ways they had never experienced. If you have been involved in sex outside of marriage and decide to appropriately discuss it with your daughter (and perhaps even your family), this positive outcome might be your experience, too.

Joe has often been asked when sex education should begin. He has almost always replied, "It starts before birth, when the child in the uterus feels Daddy hugging Mommy." This real-life answer emphasizes the truth that sex education begins when children see the relationship of their parents. They will see the way their mother and father treat each other. They learn that their mom and dad meet the everyday challenges of life—some easy and some hard, some fun and some not so fun.

Early on, of course, they will not know that their parents come together in physical intercourse. They will notice, however, a certain physicality between them by watching the hugs and kisses. One of the important things they see is that the physical relationship between their parents doesn't dominate the family's existence but integrates into all of life.

Girls can also learn how a male should relate to them by experiencing how their dad relates to them. This is one reason dad-daughter dates can be so powerful. Dads can also take a daughter on short trips, perhaps just day trips, alone. Not only does this help the "connecting" we have so emphasized, but it helps a girl know she is valuable to Dad. Dads, spending time like this with your daughter increases the chance she will marry someone like you. Girls who have a good relationship with their fathers often choose to marry guys like their fathers.[45]

Mom and Dad, try celebrating her first bra or period with a dinner out or a private party at home. This opens up the subject of sex in a natural way right at the start of these important teen years. It shows that you see the changes in your daughter and are also proud of them. It shows that you can talk naturally about physical, sexual issues with her. It starts the discussion of sex in a healthy, open way—early! Then multiple conversations can flow more easily with time.

You also need to determine, while your children are still young, how media will be used in the home. If the television is always on and you are constantly on cell phones and at the computer, it is quite natural for the children to follow the same pattern. We have already warned that media can strongly influence children's behavior. Too much media use displaces other interests, such as physical activities. It also makes it harder for parents to monitor what their children are being exposed to. Vicki Courtney has created an excellent resource titled *Logged On and Tuned Out: A Nontechie's Guide to Parenting a Tech-Savvy Generation.*[46]

> *Encourage your daughter, from the early days of puberty, to get involved in healthy activities.*

Young people are going to find exciting things to do. Their brains are wired that way. We will quote information we provided in our last book, *Hooked.* We, obviously, think it is good advice.[47]

Compelling activities must be provided for young people or, because of the way their brains are made, they will often find excitement on their own. Their brains demand the excitement of dopamine input. The diversions we provide them must be within parameters that keep them from experiencing activities that could be dangerously molding their brains to produce unhealthy behavior choices in the future, besides being dangerous to their physical health. Providing young people with interesting things to do and encouraging them to do exciting things must be understood in light of this new information, that the experiences they are having are literally molding their brains in ways that can be either beneficial or detrimental.[48] There are so many exciting activities that young people can take part in that can protect their present health and contribute to their future that it would be impossible to list them all. But the suggestions listed here can offer the dopamine high that young people are born to seek out, and help them get hooked on pursuits other than sexual activity.

We then listed academics, fine arts, athletics, and volunteer and philanthropic work as good options. There are many other healthy and exciting activities available to children. Encourage your daughter, from the early days of puberty, to get involved in healthy activities. Let's face it: They will be involved in *something*, whether good or bad.

Since we have recommended that young people not get involved sexually until they are married, we ought to consider what that message sounds like to a young person. Though (as we showed earlier) almost all young women want to get married eventually, the world in which they live constantly diminishes and criticizes the institution.[49] Glenn and Marquardt point to studies showing that the median age for women marrying for the first time rose from 20.8 years in 1970 to 25.1 years in 2000.[50]

If we are going to encourage our daughters to remain abstinent until marriage, we must provide a positive image of marriage. Obviously, the best way is by having a good marriage ourselves. But we need to also remind them that there are countless benefits in marriage. We will mention a few here. One of the best of many good books on this topic is *The Case for Marriage: Why Married People are Happier, Healthier, and Better Off Financially* by Waite and Gallagher.[51] Here are only some of the positive aspects of marriage reported in recent research. Married people:

- Are about twice as likely as single people or cohabiting couples to say they are "very happy."[52]

- Are more likely to report a highly satisfying sex life than single people who are sexually involved.[53]

- Are more faithful than those involved in other relationships.[54] In addition, 94 percent of married people in the US had only one sex partner (their spouse) in the past year.[55]

- Have more sex than sexually active unmarried people.[56]

As you pursue better communication with your daughter, you need to know that many, if not most, children will test the limits. That's because they don't really know where the limits are *until they test them*. They don't know if their parents are really serious until they challenge them. Cline and Fay note that the real world doesn't operate on punishment, but on the natural consequences of our actions.[57] Try letting your daughter experience the consequences of her

> *Many, if not most, children will test the limits. They don't really know where the limits are until they test them.*

decisions. Start applying this approach in the early teen years, if not before, to decisions that lead to consequences that do not threaten her health, safety, or future. Then, when she gets to an age where bad decisions could have severe consequences, such as driving while drinking or having premarital sex, you can hope that she will have already learned to value your opinion and make decisions accordingly.

Even if an older teen has done some things that could really hurt her future, many of the principles we have been discussing still apply. Continue "connecting" with your child. Continue showing unconditional love. Continue offering guidance. If, for example, you learn she has begun having intercourse, talk to her about "secondary virginity" (remaining abstinent from this point forward until marriage). Explain that her life is not over, and her body not worthless, just because she has had sex. You never know: Risky behavior and some of its consequences may cause her to finally listen.

These are some of the things you can do to help your daughter grow into the healthy, mature woman you both want her to be. And here's a final word: Relax. Your responsibility is great. So is your influence.

CHAPTER TEN

What Are Girls to Do?

WRITTEN DIRECTLY TO GIRLS

In the beginning of this book we have been talking to parents. This chapter is especially for girls and young women. Parents, of course, are welcome to listen in.

You are precious. There is no one else just like you. Your gifts, talents, and potential are worth celebrating. You are important not only to yourself and your family, but to the society we share and build together. Our society needs strong, healthy, and informed young women like you to succeed. However, it is not just society that has a stake in your health and well-being. You do, too! To achieve all of your goals and do great things, you know that *you* must take responsibility for your decisions and your future.

Your parents likely have been there to help you grow up. They want you to be happy and to reach your potential. If they have handed you this book, you know they care. They love you more than you can imagine and really do want what's best for you, even if you don't always understand or agree with where they're coming from.

Throughout life, though, you will encounter a lot of other people, some who will be committed to your well-being, others not so much. Some would like to make your decisions for you, tell you how you should look, whom you should imitate, and what you should do.

But, as you have probably already have found out, many of these other people do not always have *your* best interests in mind. They certainly don't bear the responsibility for how you turn out. If you fail, they may shrug their shoulders and move on, but you will be left with the consequences. This is especially true when it comes to sex. So please keep several things in mind as you make decisions in this area:

• *Remember that sex is sexist.*

When it comes to the negative consequences of sexual activity, girls easily get the worst of it. Most of the cancer from HPV occurs in women,[1] and all of the long-term effects of pelvic inflammatory disease (PID), such as infertility and pelvic pain, occur in women. When a boy gets a girl pregnant, *he* doesn't carry the baby for nine months—*she* does. And she is usually the one who takes care of the baby once it is born. Girls also seem to suffer more depression than boys do after sexual relationships are broken.[2]

These are just some of the ways that girls suffer more than boys from the bad outcomes of sex. There are many more risks than benefits to sexual activity until you are in a lifelong, faithful relationship (like marriage). Sexually transmitted infections (STIs) and pregnancy, which are both quite common, can waylay your plans and lead to much unhappiness.

> *Don't have sex with a guy just to make him happy. Your own goals, plans, and health should be your No. 1 priority.*

Nor is abortion the walk in the park you may have heard. While some people think of it as an easy way out of a difficult situation, abortion brings many problems you may not have thought about, and it always kills a baby in the uterus. And again, it is only the *woman* who undergoes an abortion—not the man. He may pay for the abortion and even go to the clinic with you. But you will be the one who risks pain, bleeding, infection and possible injury to your internal organs, making it impossible to have children when you desire them.

Because *you* will have to deal with so many of the problems that can result from sex, *you* should have the most say in the matter. Don't have sex with a guy just to make *him* happy. Your own goals, plans, and health should be your No. 1 priority.

• *Get accurate information.*

You cannot make informed decisions about your health and happiness unless you know the real risks. Besides this book, your health care provider is another good source of information about the risks of sexual activity. But be sure to go to one who agrees with your decision to remain a virgin. A number of women in their mid-twenties (one a bank vice president) transferred their medical care to Joe because their previous doctors had actually made fun of them for still being virgins.

Understand that your brain can cause you to want to do things that are not necessarily good for you. That is just the way your brain hormones work. Being physical with a guy can give you a great feeling of excitement and can even cause you to want to have sex with him. It is normal to feel like this. But just because something is "normal" does not mean it is the best thing for *you*. So when one part of your brain is telling you to have sex, remember to use a different part of your brain to make intelligent decisions about your future.

> *When one part of your brain is telling you to have sex, use a different part of your brain to make intelligent decisions about your future.*

Don't worry—you are not agreeing to miss out on all the fun of sex for the rest of your life. Once you are married, you can experience all of the excitement of sex without jeopardizing your future.

Remember that a lot of misinformation is being directed at teens and young adults. It can come from your friends, TV, magazines, and even, sometimes, your teachers. Many people fear that if they tell you how often condoms and contraceptives fail, you will be discouraged from using them (thus leaving you open to a higher risk of pregnancy). So, sometimes with the best of intentions, they don't give you all the facts, leaving many teens and young adults with the mistaken impression that contraceptives provide foolproof protection from disease and pregnancy.

- *Put yourself in the driver's seat and make decisions to ensure your health and happiness.*

Research shows that girls often agree (against their own desires) to have sex just to make their partners happy.[3, 4] Although thinking about others when making decisions is usually a good thing, this is one case when it is up to you to look out for your own health and interests first—to be a little *selfish*, in the best sense of the word.

Having sex before you are married exposes you to many risks—STIs, pregnancy, and psychological trauma. There is *no* good reason to *ever* take these risks! Let's face it: Many girls agree to have sex with a guy because they do not want to lose him or because they think he *needs* the sexual release.[5]

> Make decisions that put your own health and life goals first.

These are simply not good enough reasons to have sex! Someone who is worth your time and attention will not leave you just because you want to wait to have sex. He will not ask you to make him happy even if it makes you unhappy. He will not pressure you to take care of his sexual "needs," which are not really needs at all, but just selfish desires. You need to make decisions that put your *own* health and life goals first.

• Protect yourself.

Many girls have felt uncomfortable with how fast a guy is moving, but they are afraid (or embarrassed) to say so. If you are ever in this situation, tell him to stop right away. Your brain is giving you warning signals, and you need to *listen* to those signals and *act* on them quickly. Sometimes, a guy won't stop even after a girl asks him to. This is rape, and a girl treated this way by a guy should report it to the police. As a matter of fact, between 15 percent and 20 percent of teens and college-age girls report that they have been raped at some point in their lives.[6]

Unfortunately, very few of these girls actually report the guys who force them into sexual activity, even though it is against the law for a guy to force a girl to have sex. That's because the girls often blame themselves for letting the situation go too far.[7] So let's get this straight—*no* guy has the right to keep going once you have told him to stop. *Ever*. If you feel like a situation is heading in that direction, leave immediately. Or scream if you are unable to leave. And listen to what your brain is telling you—it is often right. But if you are *raped*—even so-called "date rape"—report it immediately.

Of course, it makes sense to avoid situations in which you will not be in control of the decision to have sex. Stay in public places. Don't go to someone's dorm room. Don't use drugs and alcohol, which can slow your responses. Forced sex often happens to girls who have been drinking and who accompany a guy to a private place.[8]

• Demand high standards (such as honesty and respect) in a mate.

Finding a good marriage partner is not easy. As a matter of fact, it can be a bumpy ride, with lots of ups and downs. But take time to figure out what you are really looking for in a partner—what is really important—

and then stick to it. It's true that building a life together can be difficult, and many marriages fail. But just because something is hard doesn't mean you shouldn't try. Sometimes the best things in life *are* hard, but

Spend some time thinking about what the "right guy" will look like for you.

they are worth the effort. Many studies indicate that marriage makes us healthier and happier,[9] and the fact is, most girls in our society want to get married at some point.[10] So spend some time thinking about what the "right guy" will look like for you.

And please note that most girls not only want marriage but also kids,[11] and marriage provides the safest place to raise kids.[12, 13] (And keep in mind that cohabiting adults have more birth control failures than single or married people[14] and thus are more likely to get pregnant, bringing kids into a less-than-ideal situation.) So figure out what qualities you would like in the father of your children and then choose someone with those qualities in mind.

Many girls today, however, don't think they should even have a serious relationship or get married until they have graduated from college and become established in their chosen careers.[15, 16] However, there are several reasons why this may not be the best decision. One is that this can be a very long path—for example, many doctors do not become established in their careers until they are well past thirty. Because such career-minded women want to interact with men but without the time commitment of a serious relationship, some of them agree to have hookups with friends and acquaintances.[17] We are not exaggerating. Sex without commitment is even the premise of the popular 2011 film *No Strings Attached*.

However, sex with casual partners is very risky, emotionally and physically, and can result in broken dreams and lost opportunities—just the opposite of what you were hoping to achieve! If you think having short, casual sexual relationships will protect your dreams of getting a great education and a successful career, please think again. You are actually putting yourself at greater risk of losing them.

By waiting to have sex until you find a supportive marriage partner, you will avoid many of the risks of sex and make its benefits more likely. And research says that married women enjoy better sex than single women,[18] so it can definitely be worth the wait.

Contrary to what you may have heard, husbands need not block your plans, either. A good one, in fact, can help you meet all of your life goals. A good husband—someone who treats you as a partner, supports you, and wants you to succeed—can actually help you reach your goals better than you could have done alone.

• Don't live with a partner unless you are married.

Many people will recommend that you live with someone before you decide to get married. They suggest that cohabitation will enable you to really get to know a potential mate's personality (including all of his nasty habits) before making a commitment. But current research says that this is a really bad idea. People who live together before they are married (or at least before they are engaged) end up having higher rates of divorce and worse relationships.[19]

Kids who are born to cohabiting parents, meanwhile, do not fare as well, either. They are both more likely to see their parents split up[20] and to be poor.[21] Marriage is the goal that most girls have set for their lives, not cohabitation.[22] So don't compromise on your future. Don't live with a man until he puts the marriage band on your finger.

• Take control of your life.

Finally, we want to encourage you to make decisions that are in your *own* best interests, especially when it comes to sex. Many girls around you, even those you may trust and look up to, will make decisions about sex that ultimately may harm their futures. It is hard to go against the flow when seemingly everybody—guys and girls—says that sex at this time of life is "normal."

> Set your own standards. You *decide what you will do and what you won't do.*

Whatever people may say, sex can be very risky—even "normal" sex. Here's just one statistic to think about: Three out of every ten girls will get pregnant by the time they are twenty.[23] You don't want to become one of them, do you? Even with birth control, sex cannot be disconnected from pregnancy. Remember, one of the purposes of sex is procreation, not just recreation. When you engage in sex, it is not a mistake or accident when pregnancy occurs.

There's a time for children, who are always blessings, but your single years are not that time. So don't do what *other* people tell you to do with *your* body. Set your own standards. *You* decide what you will do and what you won't do. Stand up for yourself and do what is best for *you*!

Eventually, we all must become responsible for our bodies and our decisions. *You* (and no one else) will have to live in your body, and with all of your memories, for however many years you have. So be true to your best ideals and make your life count—for yourself and for others. We only get one crack at this thing called life.

CHAPTER ELEVEN

Bringing It All Together

ONCE YOUR DAUGHTER was a child. At bedtime you would talk with her using affectionate tones and words. Perhaps you would pray together or read her a story. As she began to drift off, you would gently cover her with a sheet or blanket. Joe and his wife, Marion, performed this familiar ritual countless times, sometimes together and sometimes separately, for their three daughters. So did Freda and Lee. Remember the amazing sense of love and protection you felt as you looked down at that wonderful little person lying there so vulnerable and yet, because of your protection and care, so safe?

The need for parents to "cover" their girls does not stop when they reach the age when we no longer have to tuck them in. Our daughters still need our "covering" as they grow through their teen years and even into their twenties. The nature of our covering changes but is no less important. Just as they might resist going to bed when they were little, so they sometimes will fight our guidance now that they are older. But we should be just as committed to their welfare now, even though backing off might be the easiest and most comfortable route to take.

The covering we can provide now consists of our wisdom, born out of our maturity, knowledge, and experience. We provide this covering because we love them, so they will be safe and enjoy the opportunity to grow into the people they are designed to be. To give them every advantage, we seek to help them incorporate as many personal assets as possible—such as a good work ethic, honesty, education, worthy goals, and so on. We want them to fulfill their potential and to experience health, hope, and happiness.

That's why they need the cover we have talked about in this book. Yes, without our careful guidance, our daughters *may* become successful in many ways. We have all heard inspiring stories of people who have overcome dysfunctional parents or a bad home life to achieve great things.

Give her room to breathe, to grow. You want her to be independent in the best sense of the word.

But it is safe to say that this is not the preferred route to the good life. More than likely, they will not be as successful as they could have been. They may stumble into relative happiness without our guidance, but they could just as easily end up carrying a lot of unnecessary regrets into adulthood. Why would we stand by and let that happen?

Of course, the goal is to guide our children to become who *they* are meant to be according to their temperament, talents, and gifts. The goal is not for them to become who *we* think they should be.[1] We simply desire to guide them toward responsible adulthood.

This means that we are raising our children to grow into independent adults—a hard task for some of us. If we cannot gradually release our youngsters into full independence as adults, and if we constantly say things to make our child feel guilty for wanting to gradually separate during the teen years and early twenties, perhaps we need to get over it—fast. This kind of selfishness (for that's what it is) can undermine all our efforts to help our daughter become who she is supposed to be. Keeping her tied to our apron strings can severely damage both her self-esteem and her relationship with us. One of the surest ways to force her into foolish decisions is to smother her. So give her room to breathe, to grow. You want her to be independent in the best sense of the word.

The knowledge we have presented in this book will help her to become independent, able to make decisions that are in her own best interest. Remember that Francis Bacon said, "Knowledge itself is power." The world has distorted much of the available knowledge about sex, and the consequences for our young people have been devastating.

After reading this book, your "power of knowledge" will not only help your own daughter. It may even help lay the groundwork to show society a reason to follow a better way. It was Thomas Paine who said, "We have it in our power to begin the world over again." There is almost no area of society that needs to "begin over again" as much as the world of sex. *You* can be a change agent, starting in your own family.

We realize you could view *Girls Uncovered* as a very intense, overwhelming book. There are so many statistics. Attempting to digest all this information can make you feel not powerful but powerless. Yet the statistics are so consistent that we cannot avoid them or deny their validity. And if we don't take time to absorb them and communicate them clearly, we are actually failing to use powerful tools that can be of enormous help as we guide our daughters. But you don't have to be an expert. You do, however, have to care enough to equip yourself with the data. The fact that you have read this far shows that you do care.

And when we boil all this information down to its essence, the message we must share is as simple as it is devastating. The statistics show that our daughters are at incredible risk—out in the world where they live, without us. Terrible things can happen to their thoughts, attitudes, values, and behaviors. This can happen without our knowledge and certainly without our consent.

But other statistics show that we, as parents, usually have more influence on our children's thoughts, attitudes, values, and behaviors, even through the college years, than we ever thought possible. Yet given this, we must ask whether we are being the best parents possible. Are we even *being* good parents? Or are we unwittingly making mistakes that will doom our daughters?

Edward R. Murrow famously once said, "Anyone who isn't confused doesn't really understand the situation." Confusion over these vital issues produces in us a sense of unease, stress, even panic. So how are you supposed to be relaxed when raising your daughter, as we have suggested?

Dr. Benjamin Spock, in his landmark book about baby and childcare, begins the first chapter by saying, "Trust yourself. You know more than you think you know." Later he says, "The more people have studied different methods of bringing up children, the more they have come to the conclusion that what mothers and fathers instinctively feel like doing for their babies

> *Parenting is one of the highest responsibilities you will ever have, but it also affords some of life's deepest pleasures.*

is usually best after all."[2] But most of us feel as if we don't really know how to be parents. Is this really true? Are we all just wandering around blindly without proper knowledge of parenting, leading our children astray? We don't think so. Just as most humans have the ability to procreate, most of us have the built-in capacity to be a mom or a dad. It's just the way we're made. It seems that most parents, if they are honestly examining their lives and seeking the best for their children, "fit" being parents.

You don't have to force it. You can relax in the comfort of knowing you have the best interests of your children at heart. You will raise your kids on that foundation. You simply need to fit into that role. A lot of parenting will come quite naturally. We're not saying you won't need to work at it, study it, pray about it, or try and fail and try again. Parenting, to borrow a phrase from an old TV commercial, can be the toughest job you'll ever love. There will be days when you don't have any idea what to do and will feel perplexed and in over your head. But that's okay. In the broad scheme of things and through the years of parenting, you will find that you really *do* fit.

So we will say it again: *Relax!* Being uptight about parenting and with our children can cause us to bypass the fun and focus entirely on the work and responsibility. That stressful perspective turns parenting from delight to drudgery. Parenting can and should be a source of enjoyment. Parenting is one of the highest responsibilities you will ever have. But it also affords some of life's deepest pleasures.

> *Wrap your parenting in balance, good judgment, patience, and selflessness.*

You have a wonderful opportunity to raise, to know, to love your daughter. Enjoy her while she is around. She will be gone sooner than you think. The Roman poet Horace counseled, *Carpe diem*: Seize the day. As the ancient Hebrew psalmist noted, "This is the day that the Lord has made. Let us rejoice and be glad in it." Good advice, whatever we believe!

Wrap your parenting in balance, good judgment, patience, and selflessness. Just as we should not be uptight, neither should we be too loose. We need balance. We want to build into our daughters the characteristics that will help them get the most out of life. But we should do this with a light touch whenever possible.

It's a lot to consider, and one parenting size definitely does not fit all children. Spend time thinking about your calling as a mom or dad. Read a lot. Talk to friends. Discuss this book with each other. Be willing to change your methods even as you stick with your principles. There's an old saying: "When you know better, you do better." Of course, even if you do all this, there are no guarantees. You will still make mistakes, but that's okay. We strongly suspect that your daughter will survive them because she knows of your love.

Of course we hope that your daughter will not only survive but thrive. Eventually your daughter will grow up and no longer need you to tuck her in. But she will always need the covering that you are uniquely equipped to provide—a covering that will allow her to become the confident and independent young woman you both desire.

Notes

Chapter 1: Hopes, Dreams, and Fears

1. F. I. Luntz, *What Americans Really Want . . . Really: The Truth About Our Hopes, Dreams, and Fears* (New York: Hyperion, 2009), 256.

2. Norval Glenn and Elizabeth Marquardt, *Hooking Up, Hanging Out, and Hoping for Mr. Right: College Women on Mating and Dating Today* (New York: Institute of American Values, 2001). www.americanvalues.org/Hooking_Up.pdf.

3. Search Institute, *What Kids Need: Developmental Assets.* www.search-institute.org.

4. Add Health project page, UNC Carolina Population Center. www.cpc.unc.edu/ projects/addhealth/about.

5. M. D. Resnick, P. S. Bearman, R. W. Blum, et al., "Findings from the National Longitudinal Study on Adolescent Health," *Journal of the American Medical Association* 278 (1997), 823–32.

6. Luntz, 257.

7. C. M. Markham, D. Lormand, K. M. Gloppen, M. F. Peskin, B. Flores, B. Low, and L. D. House, "Connectedness as a Predictor of Sexual and Reproductive Health Outcomes for Youth," *Journal of Adolescent Health* 46 (2010), S23–S41.

8. J. Jaccard, P. J. Dittus, and V. V. Gordon, "Parent-Teen Communication About Premarital Sex: Factors Associated with the Extent of Communication," *Journal of Adolescent Research* 15 (2000), 187–208.

9. J. Bachman, L. Johnston, and P. O'Malley, *Monitoring the Future: Questionnaire Responses from the Nation's High School Seniors 2008* (Ann Arbor, MI: The Institute for Social Research, The University of Michigan, 2009). http:// monitoringthefuture.org.

10. N. E. Bell, *Graduate Enrollment and Degrees: 1998 to 2008* (Washington, DC: Council of Graduate Schools, 2009). www.cgsnet.org.

11. Association of American Medical Colleges, "US Medical School Applicants and Students 1982–83 to 2009–2010." www.aamc.org.

12. Glenn and Marquardt.

13. A. Chandra, G. M. Martinez, W. D. Mosher, J. C. Abma, and J. Jones. "Fertility, Family Planning, and Reproductive Health of US Women: Data from the 2002 National Survey of Family Growth," *Vital and Health Statistics*, 23 (2005), 1–160.

14. B. Dalton, E. Glennie, and S. J. Ingels, "Late High School Dropouts: Characteristics, Experiences, and Changes Across Cohorts," *Institute of Educational Sciences* (Washington, DC: US Department of Education, National Center for Education Statistics, 2009). http://nces.ed.gov/pubs2009/2009307.pdf.

15. T. D. Snyder, S. A. Dillow, and C. M. Hoffman, "Digest of Education Statistics 2007," *Institute of Educational Sciences* (Washington, DC: US Department of Education, National Center for Education Statistics, 2008). http://nces.ed.gov/.

16. L. Berkner and S. Choy, "Descriptive Summary of 2003-04 Beginning Postsecondary Students: Three Years Later," *Institute of Educational Sciences* (Washington, DC: US Department of Education, National Center for Education Statistics, 2008). http://nces.ed.gov/pubs2008/2008174.pdf.

17. Glenn and Marquardt.

Chapter 2: Girls: Covered or Uncovered

1. Norval Glenn and Elizabeth Marquardt, *Hooking Up, Hanging Out, and Hoping for Mr. Right: College Women on Mating and Dating Today* (New York: Institute of American Values, 2001). www.americanvalues.org.

2. Ibid.

3. J. N. Giedd, "Structural Magnetic Resonance Imaging of the Adolescent Brain," *Annals of the New York Academy of Science* 1021 (2004), 77–85.

4. Steven Mostyn, "Teens in United States Send Staggering 3,339 Text Messages per Month," *The Tech Herald* (October 18, 2010). www.thetechherald.com.

5. The National Campaign to Prevent Teen and Unplanned Pregnancy, *Sex and Tech: Results from a Survey of Teens and Young Adults* (Washington, DC: The National Campaign to Prevent Teen and Unplanned Pregnancy, 2008).

6. Janis Wolak, Kimberly Mitchell, and David Finkelhor, *Online Victimization of Youth: Five Years Later* (Alexandria, VA: National Center for Missing and Exploited Children, 2006). www.missingkids.com/en_US/publications/NC167.pdf.

7. Dale Kunkel, Keren Eyal, Keli Finnerty, Erica Biely, and Edward Donnerstein, *Sex on TV* (Menlo Park, CA: Kaiser Family Foundation, 2005). www.kff.org.

8. J. J. Arnett, "The Sounds of Sex: Sex in Teens' Music and Music Videos" in J. D. Brown, J. R. Steele, and K. Walsh-Childers, eds., *Sexual Teens, Sexual Media: Investigating Media's Influence on Adolescent Sexuality* (Mahwah, NJ: Lawrence Erlbaum, 2002), 253–64.

9. S. L. Escobar-Chaves, S. R. Tortolero, C. M. Markham, B. J. Low, P. Eitel, and P. Thickstun, "Impact of Media on Adolescent Sexual Attitudes and Behaviors," *Pediatrics* 116 (2005), 303–26.

10. V. J. Rideout, U. G. Foehr, and D. F. Roberts, *Generation M2: Media in the Lives of 8- to 18-Year Olds* (Menlo Park, CA: Kaiser Family Foundation, January 2010). www.kff.org.

11. V. C. Strasburger, A. B. Jordan, and E. Donnerstein, "Health Effects of Media on Children and Adolescents," *Pediatrics* 125 (2010), 756–67.

12. R. L. Collins, M. N. Elliott, S. H. Berry, D. E. Kanouse, D. Kunkel, S. B. Hunter, and A. Miu, "Watching Sex on Television Predicts Adolescent Initiation of Sexual Behavior," *Pediatrics* 114 (2004), 280–89.

Chapter 3: The Sexual Lives of Teens and Young Adults

1. Vigen Guroian, "Dorm Brothel: The new debauchery, and the colleges that let it happen," *Christianity Today* (February 2005). www.christianitytoday.com.

2. Centers for Disease Control and Prevention, "Youth Risk Behavior Surveillance System Overview." http://cdc.gov/HealthyYouth.

3. National Center for Health Statistics, "About the National Survey of Family Growth." www.cdc.gov/nchs/nsfg/about_nsfg.htm.

4. Centers for Disease Control and Prevention, "Youth Risk Behavior Surveillance—United States, 2009," Surveillance Summaries, *Morbidity and Mortality Weekly Report* (SS-5, 2010), 59.

5. J. D. Hans, M. Gillen, and K. Akande, "Sex Redefined: The Reclassification of Oral-Genital Contact," *Perspectives on Sexual and Reproductive Health* 42 (2010), 74–78.

6. T. Downing-Matibag and B. Geisinger, "Hooking Up and Sexual Risk-Taking Among College Students: A Health Belief Model Perspective," *Qualitative Health Research* 19 (2009), 1196–209.

7. B. Halpern-Felsher, "Oral Sexual Behavior: Harm Reduction or Gateway Behavior?" *Journal of Adolescent Health* 43 (2008), 207–8.

8. W. Mosher, A. Chandra, and J. Jones, "Sexual Behavior and Selected Health Measures: Men and Women 15–44 Years of Age, United States, 2002," *Advance Data* 362 (2005), 1–54.

9. Ibid.

10. Centers for Disease Control and Prevention, "Youth Risk Behavior Surveillance: National College Health Risk Behavior Survey—United States, 1995," CDC Surveillance Summaries, *Morbidity and Mortality Weekly Report*, (SS-6, 1997) 46.

11. American College Health Association, *American College Health Association-National College Health Assessment II: Reference Group Data Report Fall 2008* (Baltimore: American College Health Association, 2009).

12. Mosher, 1–54.

13. CDC, "Youth Risk Behavior Surveillance: National College Health Risk Behavior Survey—United States, 1995."

14. American College Health Association.

15. E. L. Paul, B. McManus, and A. Hayes. "Hookups: Characteristics and Correlates of College Students' Spontaneous and Anonymous Sexual Experiences." *Journal of Sexual Research* (2000, 37): 76–88.

16. Ibid.

17. J. C. Abma, G. M. Martinez, and C. E. Copen, "Teenagers in the United States: Sexual Activity, Contraceptive Use, and Childbearing, National Survey of Family Growth 2006–2008," National Center for Health Statistics. *Vital and Health Statistics* 23 (December, 2010), 30.

18. C. Grello, D. Welsh, M. Harper, and J. Dickson, "Dating and Sexual Relationship Trajectories and Adolescent Functioning," *Adolescent and Family Health*. 3(3) (2003), 103–12.

19. W. Manning, P. Giordano, and M. Longmore, "Hooking Up: The Relationship Contexts of 'Nonrelationship' Sex," *Journal of Adolescent Research* 21(5) (2006), 459–83.

20. C. Bradshaw, A. Kahn, and B. Saville, "To Hook Up or Date: Which Gender Benefits?" *Sex Roles* 62 (2010), 661–69.

21. Paul, et al., "Hookups," 76–88.

22. E. L. Paul and K. Hayes, "The Casualties of 'Casual' Sex: A Qualitative Exploration of the Phenomenology of College Students' Hookups," *Journal of Social and Personal Relationships* 19(5) (2002), 639–61.

23. Caitlyn Flanagan, "The Hazards of Duke: A now infamous PowerPoint presentation exposes a lot about men, women, sex, and alcohol—and about how universities are letting their female students down," *The Atlantic* (January/February, 2011). www.theatlantic.com/magazine.

24. Laura Sessions Stepp, *Unhooked: How Young Women Pursue Sex, Delay Love, and Lose at Both* (New York: Penguin Group, 2007), 113–20.

25. Downing-Matibag and Geisinger, 1196–209.

26. Paul and Hayes, 639–61.

27. CDC, "Youth Risk Behavior Surveillance—United States, 2009," 59.

28. Kaiser Family Foundation, *Virginity and the First Time: A Series of Surveys of Teens About Sex*, Publication no. 3368 (Menlo Park, CA: The Henry J. Kaiser Family Foundation, 2003). www.kff.org.

29. W. F. Flack Jr., K. A. Daubman, M. L. Caron, et al., "Risk Factors and Consequences of Unwanted Sex Among University Students: Hooking Up, Alcohol, and Stress Response," *Journal of Interpersonal Violence* 22 (2007), 139–57.

30. The National Campaign to Prevent Teen and Unplanned Pregnancy, *Sex and Tech: Results from a Survey of Teens and Young Adults* (Washington, DC: The National Campaign to Prevent Teen and Unplanned Pregnancy, 2008).

31. Mike Bunker, " 'Sexting' surprise: Teens face child porn charges," msnbc.com (January 15, 2009). www.msnbc.msn.com/id/28679588/.

Chapter 4: STIs

1. Centers for Disease Control and Prevention, "Youth Risk Behavior Surveillance —United States, 2009," Surveillance Summaries, *Morbidity and Mortality Weekly Report* SS-5 (2010), 59.

2. American College Health Association, *American College Health Association-National College Health Assessment II: Reference Group Data Report Fall 2008* (Baltimore: American College Health Association, 2009).

3. T. Downing-Matibag and B. Geisinger, "Hooking Up and Sexual Risk Taking Among College Students: A Health Belief Model Perspective," *Qualitative Health Research* 19(9) (2009), 1196–209.

4. Ibid.

5. H. Weinstock, S. Berman, and W. Cates Jr., "Sexually Transmitted Diseases among American Youth: Incidence and Prevalence Estimates, 2000" *Perspectives on Sexual and Reproductive Health* 36(1) (2004), 6–10.

6. Peter S. Bearman, James Moody, and Katherine Stovel, "Chains of Affection: The Structure of Adolescent Romantic and Sexual Networks," *American Journal of Sociology* 110 (2004), 44–91.

7. Centers for Disease Control and Prevention, *Sexually Transmitted Disease Surveillance, 2008* (Atlanta: US Department of Health and Human Services, November 2009).

8. A. N. Burchell, H. Richardson, S. M. Mahmud, et al., "Modeling the Sexual Transmissibility of Human papillomavirus Infection Using Stochastic Computer Simulation and Empirical Data from a Cohort Study of Young Women in Montreal, Canada," *American Journal of Epidemiology* 163 (2006), 534–43.

9. E. M. de Villiers, C. Fauquet, T. R. Broker, H. U. Bernard, and H. zur Hausen, "Classification of papillomaviruses," *Virology* 324 (2004), 17–27.

10. G. D. Sanders and A. V. Taira, "Cost-effectiveness of a Potential Vaccine for Human papillomavirus," *Emerging Infectious Diseases* 9(1) (2003), 37–48.

11. R. L. Winer, J. P. Hughes, Q. Feng, S. O'Reilly, N. B. Kiviat, K. K. Holmes, and L. A. Koutsky, "Condom Use and the Risk of Genital Human papillomavirus in Young Women," *New England Journal of Medicine* 354 (2006), 2645–54.

12. E. F. Dunne, E. R. Unger, M. Sternberg, G. McQuillan, D. C. Swan, S. S. Patel, and L. E. Markowitz, "Prevalence of HPV Infection among Females in the United States," *Journal of the American Medical Association* 297 (2007), 813–19.

13. J. M. Partridge, J. P. Hughes, Q. Feng, et al., "Genital Human papillomavirus Infection in Men: Incidence and Risk Factors in a Cohort of University Students," *Journal of Infectious Diseases* 196 (2007), 1128–36.

14. L. Koutsky, "Epidemiology of Genital Human papillomavirus Infection," *American Journal of Medicine* 102(5A) (1997), 3–8.

15. Rachel L. Winer, Shu-Kuang Lee, James P. Hughes, Diane E. Adam, Nancy B. Kiviat, and Laura A. Koutsky, "Genital Human papillomavirus Infection: Incidence and Risk Factors in a Cohort of Female University Students," *American Journal of Epidemiology* 157 (2003), 218–26.

16. G. Y. Ho, R. Bierman, L. Beardsley, C. J. Chang, and R. D. Burk, "National History of Cervicovaginal papillomavirus in Young Women," *New England Journal of Medicine* 338(7) (1998), 423–28.

17. A. K. Chaturvedi, "Beyond Cervical Cancer: Burden of Other HPV-Related Cancers among Men and Women," *Journal of Adolescent Health* 46(4 Supplement) (2010), S20–S26.

18. National Cancer Institute, *Fact Sheet: Pap Test* (Bethesda, MD: National Cancer Institute, September 2, 2009). www.cancer.gov/cancertopics.

19. Read more about Pap smears and STIs at www.righthealth.com/topic/Acog_Guidelines/overview.

20. World Health Organization (HPV Information Centre), "Human papillomavirus and Related Cancers in World," *Summary Report Update, November 15, 2010.* http://apps.who.int/hpvcentre.

21. WHO/ICO Information Centre on HPV and Cervical Cancer, "Human Papillomavirus and Related Cancers in United States of America, *Summary Report 2010.* www.who.int/hpvcentre/en.

22. Chaturvedi, "Beyond Cervical Cancer."

23. C. Y. Kan, B. J. Iacopetta, J. S. Lawson, and N. J. Whitaker, "Identification of Human papillomavirus DNA Gene Sequences in Human Breast Cancer," *British Journal of Cancer* 93 (2005), 946–48.

24. Y. Yu, T. Morimoto, M. Sasa, et al., "Human papillomavirus Type 33 DNA in Breast Cancer in Chinese," *Breast Cancer* 7 (2000), 33–36.

25. S. Shukla, A. C. Bharti, S. Mahata, S. Hussain, R. Kumar, S. Hedau, and B. C. Das, "Infection of Human papillomaviruses in Cancers of Different Human Organ Sites," *Indian Journal of Medical Research* 130 (2009), 222–33.

26. G. M. Clifford, J. S. Smith, M. Plummer, N. Munoz, and S. Franceschi, "Human papillomavirus types in invasive cervical cancer analysis," *British Journal of Cancer* 88 (January 2003), 63–73.

27. J. S. Smith, L. Lindsay, B. Hoots, et al., "Human papillomavirus type distribution in invasive cervical cancer and high-grade cervical lesions: a meta-analysis update," *International Journal of Cancer* 121(3) (2007), 621–32.

28. Katherin U. Jansen and Alan R. Shaw, "Human papillomavirus Vaccines and Prevention of Cervical Cancer," *Annual Review of Medicine* 55 (2004), 319–31.

29. Smith, et al.

30. Center for Disease Control and Prevention, "FDA Licensure of bivalent humanpapilloma virus (HPV2, Cervarix) for use in females and updated HPV vaccination recommendations from the Advisory Committee on Immunization Practices (ACIP), *Morbidity and Mortality Weekly Report* 59(20) (2010), 626–29.

31. Ralph P. Insinga, Erik J. Dasbach, and Evan R. Myers, "The Health and Economic Burden of Genital Warts in a Set of Private Health Plans in the United States," *Clinical Infectious Diseases* 36 (2003), 1397–403.

32. Robert D. Burk, Gloria Y. F. Ho, Leah Beardsley, Michele Lempa, Michael Peters and Robert Bierman, "Sexual Behavior and Partner Characteristics Are the Predominant Risk Factors for Genital Human papillomavirus Infection in Young Women," *Journal of Infectious Diseases* 174 (1996), 679–89.

33. N. S. Murthy and A. Mathew, "Risk Factors for Pre-cancerous Lesions of the Cervix," *European Journal of Cancer Prevention* 9 (2000), 5–14.

34. Ibid.

35. Winer, et al., "Genital Human papillomavirus Infection."

36. Ibid.

37. M. Schiffman and P. E. Castle, "Human papillomavirus: Epidemiology and Public Health," *The Archives of Pathology & Laboratory Medicine* 127 (2003), 930–34.

38. Centers for Disease Control and Prevention, "Sexually Transmitted Disease Surveillance, 2008."

39. Weinstock, et al.

40. Centers for Disease Control and Prevention, "Sexually Transmitted Disease Surveillance, 2008."

41. E. L. Korenromp, M. K. Sudaryo, S. J. de Vlas, et al., "What Proportion of Episodes of Gonorrhoea and Chlamydia Becomes Symptomatic?" *International Journal of STD & AIDS* 13 (2002), 91–101.

42. L. Westrom, R. Joesoef, G. Reynolds, A. Hagdu, and S. E. Thompson, "Pelvic Inflammatory Disease and Fertility: A Cohort Study of 1,844 Women with Laparoscopically Verified Disease and 657 Control Women with Normal Laparoscopic Results," *Sexually Transmitted Diseases* 19 (1992), 185–92.

43. Centers for Disease Control and Prevention, "Sexually Transmitted Diseases Treatment Guidelines, 2006," *Morbidity and Mortality Weekly Report* 55 (RR-11) (2006), 1–94. www.cdc.gov.

44. Weinstock, et al.

45. Korenromp, et al.

46. Centers for Disease Control and Prevention, *Sexually Transmitted Disease Surveillance, 2008* (Atlanta: US Department of Health and Human Services, November 2009).

47. Weinstock, et al.

48. R. L. Ashley and A. Wald, "Genital Herpes: Review of the Epidemic and Potential Use of Type-specific Serology," *Clinical Microbiology Reviews* 12(1) (1999), 1–8.

49. Centers for Disease Control and Prevention, "Seroprevalence of Herpes Simplex Virus Type 2 Among Persons Aged 14–49 years—United States, 2005-2008," *Morbidity and Mortality Weekly Report* 59 (2010), 456–59.

50. O. Carney, E. Ross, C. Bunker, et al., "A Prospective Study of the Psychological Impact on Patients with a First Episode of Genital Herpes," *Genitourinary Medicine* 70 (1994), 40–45.

51. S. Drake, S. Taylor, D. Brown, and D. Pillay, "Regular Review: Improving the Care of Patients with Genital Herpes," *British Medical Journal* 321 (2000), 619–23.

52. Carney, et al.

53. H. I. Hall, R. Song, P. Rhodes, et al., "Estimation of HIV Incidence in the United States," *Journal of the American Medical Association* 300 (2008), 520–29.

54. H. I. Hall, Q. An, A. B. Hutchinson, and S. Sansom, "Estimating the Lifetime Risk of a Diagnosis of the HIV Infection in 33 States, 2004–2005," *Journal of Acquired Immune Deficiency Syndromes* 49 (2008), 294–97.

55. E. M Gardner, M. E. Maravi, C. Rietmeijer, A. J. Davidson, and W. J. Burman, "The Association of Adherence to Antiretroviral Therapy with Healthcare Utilization and Costs for Medical Care," *Applied Health Economics and Health Policy* 6 (2008), 145–55.

56. Centers for Disease Control and Prevention, *The National Plan to Eliminate Syphilis from the United States* (Atlanta: US Department of Health and Human Services, October 1999). www.cdc.gov/stopsyphilis/Plan.pdf.

57. CDC, "Sexually Transmitted Disease Surveillance, 2008."

58. K. K. Holmes, P. F. Sparling, W. E. Stamm, et al., "Introduction and Overview," *Sexually Transmitted Diseases*, 4th ed. (New York: McGraw-Hill Medical, 2008), xvii, xxiii.

59. American Cancer Society, *Cervical Cancer Guide* (Atlanta: American Cancer Society, 2009). www.cancer.org.

60. National Institute of Allergy and Infectious Diseases, "Workshop Summary: Scientific Evidence on Condom Effectiveness for Sexually Transmitted Disease (STD) Prevention, July 20, 2001," National Institutes of Health, Department of Health and Human Services. www.nih.gov.

Chapter 5: Pregnancy

1. K. Kost, S. Henshaw, and L. Carlin, *US Teenage Pregnancies, Births and Abortions: National and State Trends and Trends by Race and Ethnicity* (New York: Guttmacher Institute, 2010). www.guttmacher.org.

2. The National Campaign to Prevent Teen and Unplanned Pregnancy, "Fact Sheet: How Is the 3 in 10 Statistic Calculated?" (Washington, DC: The National Campaign to Prevent Teen and Unplanned Pregnancy, 2008). www.thenationalcampaign.org.

3. S. D. Hoffman and R. A. Maynard, "The Study, the Context, and the Findings in Brief," *Kids Having Kids: Economic Costs & Social Consequences of Teen Pregnancy,* 2nd ed. (Washington, DC: The Urban Institute Press, 2008), 1–3.

4. V. J. Hotz, S. W. McElroy, and S. G. Sanders, "Consequences of Teen Child-

bearing through 1993" in S. D. Hoffman and R. A. Maynard, eds., *Kids Having Kids: Economic Costs and Social Consequences of Teen Pregnancy*, 2nd ed. (Washington, DC: The Urban Institute Press, 2008), 56.

5. X. K. Chen, S. W. Wen, N. Fleming, K. Demissie, G. G. Rhoads, and M. Walker, "Teenage Pregnancy and Adverse Birth Outcomes: A Large Population Based Retrospective Cohort Study," *International Journal of Epidemiology* 36 (2007), 368–73.

6. A. J. Cunnington, "What's So Bad about Teenage Pregnancy?" *Journal of Family Planning and Reproductive Health* 27 (2001), 36–41.

7. R. A. Maynard, *Kids Having Kids: A Robin Hood Foundation Special Report on the Costs of Adolescent Childbearing* (New York: The Robin Hood Foundation, 1996).

8. J. S. Manlove, E. Terry-Humen, L. A. Mincieli, and K. A. Moore, "Outcomes for Children of Teen Mothers from Kindergarten through Adolescence" in S. D. Hoffman and R.A. Maynard, eds., *Kids Having Kids: Economic Costs and Social Consequences of Teen Pregnancy*, 2nd ed. (Washington, DC: The Urban Institute Press, 2008), 182–83.

9. Robert M. George, Allen Harden, and B. J. Lee, "Consequences of Teen Childbearing for Child Abuse, Neglect, and Foster Care Placement," in S. D. Hoffman and R.A. Maynard, eds., *Kids Having Kids: Economic Costs and Social Consequences of Teen Pregnancy*, 2nd ed. (Washington, DC: The Urban Institute Press, 2008), 276–78.

10. R. Haveman, B. Wolfe, and E. Peterson, "Children of Teen Mothers as Young Adults" in S. D. Hoffman and R. A. Maynard, eds. *Kids Having Kids: Economic Costs and Social Consequences of Teen Pregnancy*, 2nd ed. (Washington, DC: The Urban Institute Press, 2008), 330–32.

11. J. Grogger, "Consequences for Incarceration among Adult Children" in S. D. Hoffman and R. A. Maynard, eds., *Kids Having Kids: Economic Costs and Social Consequences of Teen Pregnancy*, 2nd ed. (Washington, DC: The Urban Institute Press, 2008), 294–302.

12. R. A. Maynard and S. D. Hoffman, "The Costs of Adolescent Childbearing," in S. D. Hoffman and R. A. Maynard, eds., *Kids Having Kids: Economic Costs and Social Consequences of Teen Pregnancy*, 2nd ed. (Washington, DC: The Urban Institute Press, 2008), 381.

13. Manlove, et al., 185–87.

14. B. E. Hamilton, J. A. Martin, and S. J. Ventura, "Births: Preliminary Data for 2008," *National Vital Statistics Reports* 58(16) (2010), 1–18.

15. S. J. Ventura and C. A. Bachrach, "Nonmarital Childbearing in the United States, 1940-99," *National Vital Statistics Reports* 48(16) (2000), 1–40.

16. Hamilton, et al.

17. Kost, et al.

18. J. C. Abma, G. M. Martinez, and C. E. Copen, "Teenagers in the United States: Sexual Activity, Contraceptive Use, and Childbearing," National Survey of Family Growth 2006-2008, *Vital and Health Statistics* 23 (2010), 30.

19. Ibid.

20. J. C. Abma, G. M. Martinez, W. D. Mosher, and B. S. Dawson, "Teenagers in the United States: Sexual Activity, Contraceptive Use, and Childbearing, 2002," National Center for Health Statistics, *Vital and Health Statistics* 23 (2004), 24.

21. K. Kaye, K. Sullentrop, and C. Sloup, *The Fog Zone: How Misperceptions, Magical Thinking, and Ambivalence Put Young Adults at Risk for Unplanned Pregnancy* (Washington, DC: The National Campaign to Prevent Teen and Unplanned Pregnancy, 2009), 31.

22. R. A. Crosby, S. A. Sanders, W. L. Yarber, C. A. Graham, and B. Dodge, "Condom Use Errors and Problems Among College Men," *Sexually Transmitted Diseases* 29 (2002), 552–57.

23. K. Kost, S. Singh, B. Vaughan, J. Trussell, and A. Bankole, "Estimates of Contraceptive Failure from the 2002 National Survey of Family Growth," *Contraception* 77 (2008), 10–21.

24. Ibid.

Chapter 6: Emotional Attachment

1. R. Johnson, K. Browne, and C. Hamilton-Giachritsis, "Young Children in Institutional Care at Risk of Harm," *Trauma, Violence & Abuse* 7 (1) (2006), 34–60.

2. J. A. Coan, H. S. Schaefer, and R. J. Davidson, "Lending a Hand: Social Regulation of the Neural Response to Threat," *Psychological Science* 17 (2006), 1032–39.

3. Commission on Children at Risk, *Hardwired to Connect: The New Scientific Case for Authoritative Communities* (New York: Institute for American Values, 2003), 17.

4. Ibid.

5. Ibid., 16.

6. H. J. Lee, A. H. Macbeth, J. H. Pagani, and W. S. Young III, "Oxytocin: The Great Facilitator of Life," *Progress in Neurobiology* 88 (2009), 127–51.

7. K. Uvnas-Moberg, "Oxytocin May Mediate the Benefits of Positive Social Interaction and Emotions," *Psychoneuroendocrinology* 23 (1998), 819–35.

8. R. Feldman, A. Weller, O. Zagoory-Sharon, and A. Levine, "Evidence for a Neuroendocrineological Foundation of Human Affiliation: Plasma Oxytocin Levels Across Pregnancy and the Postpartum Period Predict Mother-Infant Bonding," *Psychological Science* 18 (2007), 965–70.

9. Dr. Jim Reynolds, associate professor of geology, Brevard College, NC, personal communication.

10. D. Goleman, *Social Intelligence: The New Science of Human Relationships* (New York: Bantam Dell, 2006), 42.

11. F. A. Champagne, "Epigenetic Mechanisms and the Transgenerational Effects of Maternal Care," *Frontiers in Neuroendocrinology* 29 (2008), 386–97.

12. R. A. Turner, M. Altemus, T. Enos, B. Cooper, and T. McGuinness, "Preliminary Research on Plasma Oxytocin in Normal Cycling Women: Investigating Emotion and Interpersonal Distress," *Psychiatry* 62 (1999), 97–113.

13. K. C. Light, K. M. Grewan, and J. A. Amico, "More Frequent Partner Hugs and Higher Oxytocin Levels Are Linked to Lower Blood Pressure and Heart Rate in Premenopausal Women," *Biological Psychology* 69 (2005), 5–21.

14. C. S. Carter, "Oxytocin and Sexual Behavior," *Neuroscience and Biobehavioral Reviews* 16 (1992), 131–44.

15. R. T. Michael, J. H. Gagnon, E. O. Laumann, and G. Kolata, *Sex in America: A Definitive Survey* (New York: Little, Brown and Company, 1994), 105.

16. W. B. Wilcox, W. J. Doherty, H. Fisher, et al., *Why Marriage Matters, Twenty-six Conclusions from the Social Sciences*, 2nd ed. (New York: Institute for American Values, 2005).

17. M. Kosfeld, M. Heinrichs, P. J. Zak, U. Fischbacher, and E. Fehr, "Oxytocin Increases Trust in Humans," *Nature* 435 (2005), 673–76.

18. T. Baumgartner, M. Heinrichs, A. Vonlanthen, U. Fischbacher, E. Fehr, "Oxytocin Shapes the Neural Circuitry of Trust and Trust Adaptation in Humans," *Neuron* 58 (2008), 639–50.

19. Louanne Brizendine, *The Female Brain* (New York: Morgan Road Books, 2006), 68.

20. D. R. Weinberger, B. Elvevag, J. N. Giedd, *The Adolescent Brain: A Work in Progress* (Washington, DC: The National Campaign to Prevent Teen Pregnancy, 2005), 12.

21. J. N. Giedd, "Structural Magnetic Resonance Imaging of the Adolescent Brain," *Annals of the New York Academy of Science* 1021 (2004), 77–85.

22. J. N. Giedd, "The Teen Brain: Insights from Neuroimaging," *Journal of Adolescent Health* 42 (2008), 335–43.

23. T. Elbert, C. Pantev, C. Wienbruch, B. Rochstroh, and E. Taub, "Increased Cortical Representation of the Left Hand of String Players," *Science* 270 (1995), 305–7.

24. Weinberger, et. al., 12.

25. Brizendine, 18–19.

26. H. E. Fisher, "Lust, Attraction, and Attachment in Mammalian Reproduction," *Human Nature* 9 (1998), 23–52.

27. K. M. Durante and N. P. Li, "Oestradiol Level and Opportunistic Mating in Women," *Biology Letters* 5 (2009), 179–82.

28. S. Richard and H. H. Zingg, "The Human Oxytocin Gene Promoter Is Regulated by Estrogens," *The Journal of Biological Chemistry* 265 (1990), 6098–103.

29. Carter, 131–44.

30. O. Arias-Carrion and E. Poppel, "Dopamine, Learning, and Reward-Seeking Behavior," *Acta Neurobiologiae Experimentalis* 67 (2007), 481–88.

31. M. K. McClintock, S. Bullivant, S. Jacob, N. Spencer, B. Zelano, and C. Ober, "Human Body Scents: Conscious Perceptions and Biological Effects," *Chemical Senses* 30 (2005), i135–i137.

32. M. F. Bhutta, "Sex and the Nose: Human Pheromonal Responses," *Journal of the Royal Society of Medicine* 100 (2007), 268–74.

33. J. Havlicek, S. C. Roberts, and J. Flegr, "Women's Preference for Dominant Male Odour: Effects of Menstrual Cycle and Relationship Status," *Biology Letters* 1 (2005), 256–59.

34. K. Grammer, B. Fink, and N. Neave, "Human Pheromones and Sexual Attraction," *European Journal of Obstetrics and Gynecology and Reproductive Biology* 118 (2005), 135–42.

35. C. Koch, *Biophysics of Computation: Information Processing in Single Neuron* (New York: Oxford University Press, 1999), 87.

36. J. N. Giedd, "The Anatomy of Mentalization: A View from Developmental Neuroimaging," *Bulletin of the Menninger Clinic* 67 (2003), 132–42.

37. Weinberger, et. al., 2.

38. Ibid., 12.

39. The National Campaign to Prevent Teen and Unplanned Pregnancy, *That's What He Said: What Guys Think About Sex, Love, Contraception, and Relationships* (Washington, DC: The National Campaign to Prevent Teen and Unplanned Pregnancy, 2010).

40. "Hookup Survey Results," *Seventeen* Magazine (2006). www.seventeen.com.

41. The National Campaign to Prevent Teen and Unplanned Pregnancy.

42. D. D. Hallfors, M. W. Waller, D. Bauer, C. A. Ford, and C. T. Halpern, "Which Comes First in Adolescence—Sex and Drugs or Depression?" *American Journal of Preventive Medicine* 29 (2005), 163–70.

43. R. E. Rector, K. A. Johnson, and L. R. Noyes, *Sexually Active Teenagers Are More Likely to Be Depressed and to Attempt Suicide* (Washington, DC: The Heritage Center for Data Analysis, The Heritage Foundation, Publication CDA03–04, 2003).

44. R. Finger, T. Thelen, J. Vessey, J. Mohn, and J. Mann, "Association of Virginity at Age 18 with Educational Economic, Social, and Health Outcomes in Middle Adulthood," *Adolescent and Family Health* 3 (2004), 164–70.

45. American College Health Association, *American College Health Association-National College Health Assessment II: Reference Group Data Report Fall 2008* (Baltimore: American College Health Association, 2009), 31–33. www.acha-ncha.org.

46. N. I. Eisenberger and M. C. Lieberman, "Why Rejection Hurts: A Common Neural Alarm System for Physical and Social Pain," *Cognitive Science* 8 (2004), 294–300.

47. H. E Fisher, L. L. Brown, A. Aron, G. Strong, and D. Mashek, "Reward, Rejection, and Emotion Regulation Systems Associated with Rejection in Love," *Journal of Neurophysiology* 104 (2010), 51–60.

48. R. E. Rector, K. A. Johnson, L. R. Noyes, and S. Martin, *The Harmful Effects of Early Sexual Activity and Multiple Sexual Partners Among Women: A Book of Charts* (Washington, DC: The Heritage Foundation, 2003), 4.

49. T. B. Heaton, "Factors Contributing to Increasing Marital Stability in the United States," *Journal of Family Issues* 23 (2002), 392–409.

50. J. R. Kahn and K. A. London, "Premarital Sex and the Risk of Divorce," *Journal of Marriage and Family* 53 (1991), 845–55.

51. S. S. Janus and C. L. Janus, *The Janus Report on Sexual Behavior* (New York: John Wiley & Sons, Inc., 1993), 175–76.

52. "Delaying sex might strengthen marriage," *Health Daily News* (December, 2010). www.babycenter.com.

53. L. F. Salazar, R. J. DiClemente, G. M. Wingwood, R. A. Crosby, D. L. Lang, and K. Harrington, "Biologically Confirmed Sexually Transmitted Infection and Depressive Symptomatology Among African-American Female Adolescents," *Sexually Transmitted Infection* 82 (2006), 55–60.

54. L. A. Shrier, S. K. Harris, and W. R. Beardslee, "Temporal Associations Between Depressive Symptoms and Self-Reported Sexually Transmitted Disease Among Adolescents," *Archives of Pediatric and Adolescent Medicine* 156 (2002), 599–606.

55. See chapter 1.

56. The U.S Department of Education reports that about 6 percent of girls drop out of high school. Of these, 28 percent say pregnancy and 25 percent say motherhood was the cause. Of the eighteen- to twenty-four-year-old females who successfully completed high school, less than 50 percent are enrolled in college. Of those who do enroll in a four-year program, about 17 percent drop out within two to three years. "Personal reasons," cited by over 60 percent of these girls, is by far the most common reason given for dropping out of college. Obviously, some of these personal reasons were pregnancy, but some also may have been the depression resulting from sexual liaisons.

57. J. G. Silverman, A. Raj, and K. Clements, "Dating violence and associated risk and pregnancy among adolescent girls in the United States," *Pediatrics* 114(2) (2004), 220–57.

58. R. T. Michael, J. H. Gagnon, E. O. Laumann, and G. Kolata, *Sex in America: A Definitive Survey* (New York: Little, Brown and Company, 1994), 105-6.

59. Ibid.

Chapter 7: How Society Misleads Girls

1. J. N. Giedd, J. Blumenthal, N. O. Jeffries, et al., "Brain Development During Childhood and Adolescence: A Longitudinal MRI Study," *Nature Neuroscience* 2 (1999), 861–63.

2. J. N. Giedd, "The Anatomy of Mentalization: A View from Developmental Neuroimaging," *Bulletin of the Menninger Clinic* 67 (2003), 132–42.

3. Ibid.

4. M. Epstein, J. P. Calzo, A. P. Smiler, and L. M. Ward, "Anything from Making Out to Having Sex: Men's Negotiations of Hooking Up and Friends with Benefits Scripts," *Journal of Sex Research* 46 (2009), 414–24.

5. The National Campaign to Prevent Teen and Unplanned Pregnancy, *That's What He Said: What Guys Think About Sex, Love, Contraception, and Relationships* (Washington, DC: The National Campaign to Prevent Teen and Unplanned Pregnancy, 2010).

6. For example, see Mark Regnerus and Jeremy Uecker, *Premarital Sex in America: How Young Americans Meet, Mate, and Think about Marrying* (New York: Oxford University Press, 2011).

7. A. Fenigstein and M. Preston, "The Desired Number of Sexual Partners as a Function of Gender, Sexual Risks, and the Meaning of 'Ideal,'" *Journal of Sex Research* 44 (2007), 89–95.

8. D. P. Schmidt, "Universal Sex Differences in the Desire for Sexual Variety: Tests from 52 Nations, 6 Continents, and 13 Islands," *Journal of Personality and Social Psychology* 85 (2003), 85–104.

9. Ibid.

10. Ibid.

11. R. T. Michael, J. H. Gagnon, E. O. Laumann, and G. Kolata, *Sex in America: A Definitive Survey* (New York: Little, Brown and Company, 1994), 93.

12. E. A. Impett and L. A. Peplau, "Sexual Compliance: Gender, Motivational, and Relationship Perspectives," *The Journal of Sex Research* 40 (2003), 87–100.

13. C. E. Kaestle, "Sexual Insistence and Disliked Sexual Activities in Young Adulthood: Differences by Gender and Relationship Characteristics," *Perspectives on Sexual and Reproductive Health* 41 (2009), 33–39.

14. B. Albert, *With One Voice 2004: America's Adults and Teens Sound Off About Teen Pregnancy* (Washington DC: The National Campaign to Prevent Teen and Unplanned Pregnancy, 2004). www.thenationalcampaign.org.

15. C. M. Grello, D. P. Welsh, and M. S. Harper, "No Strings Attached: The Nature of Casual Sex in College Students," *The Journal of Sex Research* 42 (2006), 255–67.

16. E. L. Paul and K. Hayes, "The Casualties of 'Casual' Sex: A Qualitative Exploration of the Phenomenology of College Students' Hookups," *Journal of Social and Personal Relationships* 19 (2002), 639–61.

17. Ibid.

18. D. D. Hallfors, M. W. Waller, D. Bauer, C. A. Ford, and C. T. Halpern, "Which Comes First in Adolescence—Sex and Drugs or Depression?" *American Journal of Preventive Medicine* 29 (2005), 163–70.

19. Grello, et al.

20. R. E. Rector, K. A. Johnson, and L. R. Noyes, *Sexually Active Teenagers Are More Likely to Be Depressed and to Attempt Suicide* (Washington, DC: The Heritage

Center for Data Analysis, The Heritage Foundation, Publication CDA03–04, 2003).

21. Hallfors, et al.

22. A. Lavinthal and J. Rozler, *The Hookup Handbook: A Single Girl's Guide to Living It Up* (New York: Simon Spotlight Entertainment, 2005), 54–58.

23. Ibid., 232.

24. M. Moore, *The Supergirl Dilemma: Girls Grapple with the Mounting Pressure of Expectations* (New York: Girls Incorporated, 2006).

25. E. L. Zurbriggen, R. L. Collins, S. Lamb, T. A. Roberts, D. L. Tolman, L. M. Ward, and J. Blake, *Report of the APA Task Force on the Sexualization of Girls* (Washington, DC: American Psychological Association, 2007). www.apa.org.

26. *Cosmopolitan* Magazine, cover of July 2010 issue. www.cosmopolitan.com/ celebrity/exclusive/july-cosmo-shakira.

27. J. Bachman, L. Johnston, and P. O'Malley, *Monitoring the Future: Questionnaire Responses from the Nation's High School Seniors* (Ann Arbor, MI: The Institute for Social Research, The University of Michigan, 2009). http://monitoringthefuture. org.

28. Lavinthal and Rozler, 9.

29. N. Glenn and E. Marquardt, *Hooking Up, Hanging Out, and Hoping for Mr. Right: College Women on Mating and Dating Today* (New York: Institute of American Values, 2001). www.americanvalues.org/Hooking_Up.pdf.

30. J. W. LaBrie, J. Cail, J. F. Hummer, A. Lac, and C. Neighbors, "What Men Want: The Role of Reflective Opposite-Sex Preferences in Alcohol Use Among College Women," *Psychology of Addictive Behaviors* 23 (2009), 157–62.

31. Laura Sessions Stepp, *Unhooked: How Young Women Pursue Sex, Delay Love, and Lose at Both* (New York: Riverhead Books, 2007), 117.

32. K. A. Bogle, *Hooking Up: Sex, Dating, and Relationships on Campus* (New York: New York University Press, 2008), 47, 63.

33. Lavinthal and Rozler, 11–12.

34. Glenn and Marquardt.

35. D. Popenoe, *Cohabitation, Marriage, and Child Well-being: A Cross-National Perspective* (Piscataway, NJ: The National Marriage Project, Rutgers, The State University of New Jersey, 2008), 2–4.

36. P. Y. Goodwin, W. D. Mosher, and A. Chandra, "Marriage and Cohabitation in the United States: A Statistical Portrait Based on Cycle 6 (2002) of the National Survey of Family Growth," National Center for Health Statistics, *Vital and Health Statics* 23 (2010), 8.

37. T. B. Heaton, "Factors Contributing to Increasing Marital Stability in the United States," *Journal of Family Issues* 23 (2002), 392–409.

38. G. K. Rhoades, S. M. Stanley, and H. J. Markman, "The Pre-Engagement Cohabitation Effect: A Replication and Extension of Previous Findings," *Journal of Family Psychology* 23 (2009), 107–11.

39. Ibid.

40. W. D. Manning and S. Brown, "Children's Economic Well-being in Married and Cohabiting Parent Families," *Journal of Marriage and Family* 68 (2006), 345–62.

41. C. Osborne, W. D. Manning, and P. J. Stock, "Married and Cohabiting Parents' Relationship Stability: A Focus on Race and Ethnicity," *Journal of Marriage and Family* 69 (2007), 1345–66.

42. K. Kost, S. Singh, B. Vaughan, J. Trussell, and A. Bankole, "Estimates of Contraceptive Failure from the 2002 National Survey of Family Growth," *Contraception* 77 (2008), 10–21.

43. Goodwin, et al.

44. L. J. Waite, "Does Marriage Matter?" *Demography* 32 (1995), 483–507.

Chapter 8: What Is Society to Do?

1. D. R. Weinberger, B. Elvevag, and J. N. Giedd, *The Adolescent Brain: A Work in Progress* (Washington, DC: The National Campaign to Prevent Teen Pregnancy, 2005), 12.

2. Commission on Children at Risk, *Hardwired to Connect: The New Scientific Case for Authoritative Communities* (New York: Institute for American Values, 2003), 34–35.

3. E. F. Dunne, E. R. Unger, M. Sternberg, G. McQuillan, D. C. Swan, S. S. Patel, and L. E. Markowitz, "Prevalence of HPV Infection among Females in the United States, *Journal of the American Medical Association* 297 (2007), 813–19.

4. The National Campaign to Prevent Teen and Unplanned Pregnancy, *Fact Sheet: How Is the 3 in 10 Statistic Calculated?* (Washington, DC: The National Campaign to Prevent Teen and Unplanned Pregnancy, 2008). www.thenationalcampaign.org.

5. T. B. Heaton, "Factors Contributing to Increasing Marital Stability in the United States," *Journal of Family Issues* 23 (2002), 392–409.

6. G. K. Rhoades, S. M. Stanley, and H. J. Markman, "The Pre-Engagement Cohabitation Effect: A Replication and Extension of Previous Findings," *Journal of Family Psychology* 23 (2009), 107–11.

7. K. Kost, S. Singh, B. Vaughan, J. Trussell, and A. Bankole, "Estimates of Contraceptive Failure from the 2002 National Survey of Family Growth," *Contraception* 77 (2008), 10–21.

8. C. Osborne, W. D. Manning, and P. J. Stock, "Married and Cohabiting Parents' Relationship Stability: A Focus on Race and Ethnicity," *Journal of Marriage and Family* 69 (2007), 1345–66.

9. W. D. Manning and S. Brown, "Children's Economic Well-being in Married

and Cohabiting Parent Families," *Journal of Marriage and Family* 68 (2006), 345–62.

10. P. Y. Goodwin, W. D. Mosher, and A. Chandra, "Marriage and Cohabitation in the United States: A Statistical Portrait Based on Cycle 6 (2002) of the National Survey of Family Growth," National Center for Health Statistics, *Vital and Health Statics* 23 (2010), 8.

11. S. M. Platek and D. Singh, "Optimal Waist-to-Hip Ratios in Women Activate Neural Reward Centers in Men," PLoS One 2010; 5:e9042. www.plosone.org.

12. M. Moore, *The Supergirl Dilemma: Girls Grapple with the Mounting Pressure of Expectations* (New York: Girls Incorporated, 2006).

13. Teen Choice. www.teenchoiceawards.com.

14. Ibid.

15. Lady Gaga website. www.ladygaga.com.

16. *GQ* Magazine. www.gq.com/magazine.

17. V. J. Rideout, U. G. Foehr, and D. F. Roberts, *Generation M2: Media in the Lives of 8-18 Year Olds* (Menlo Park, CA: Kaiser Family Foundation, 2010). www.kff.org.

18. E. L. Zurbriggen, R. L. Collins, S. Lamb, T. A. Roberts, D. L. Tolman, L. M. Ward, and J. Blake, *Report of the APA Task Force on the Sexualization of Girls* (Washington, DC: American Psychological Association, 2007), 2. www.apa.org.

19. MSN website. http://today.msnbc.msn.com/id/34858102/.

20. Ibid.

21. Bratz. www.bratz.com.

22. Zurbriggen, et al, 39.

23. Ibid.

24. Ibid.

25. L. Rew and Y. J. Wong, "A Systematic Review of Associations Among Religiosity/Spirituality and Adolescent Health Attitudes and Behaviors," *Journal of Adolescent Health* 38 (2006), 433–42.

26. S. Cotton, K. Zebracki, S. L. Rosenthal, J. Tsevat, and D. Drotar, "Religion/Spirituality and Adolescent Health Outcomes: A Review," *Journal of Adolescent Health* 38 (2006), 472–80.

27. Rew and Wong.

28. Commission on Children at Risk, *Hardwired*, 29–31.

29. Laura Sessions Stepp, *Unhooked: How Young Women Pursue Sex, Delay Love, and Lose at Both* (New York: Riverhead Books, 2007), 217.

30. N. Rockler-Gladen, "Coed Dorm Life: Pros and Cons of Mixed-Sex Residence Halls for College Students" (Suite101.com, March 18, 2007). www.suite101.com/content/coed-dorms-a16571.

31. Ibid.

32. The Medical Institute, organizational research.

33. V. C. Strasburger, A. B. Jordan, and E. Donnerstein, "Health Effects of Media on Children and Adolescents," *Pediatrics* 125 (2010), 756–67.

34. Zurbriggen, et al., 24.

35. B. Albert, *With One Voice 2007: America's Adults and Teens Sound Off About Teen Pregnancy* (Washington, DC: The National Campaign to Prevent Teen Pregnancy, 2007).

36. The National Campaign to Prevent Teen and Unplanned Pregnancy, *That's What He Said: What Guys Think About Sex, Love, Contraception, and Relationships* (Washington, DC: The National Campaign to Prevent Teen and Unplanned Pregnancy, 2010).

37. Shmuley Boteach, *Kosher Sex: A Recipe for Passion and Intimacy* (New York: Doubleday, 1999), 271–72.

Chapter 9: What Are Parents to Do?

1. M. D. Resnick, P. S. Bearman, R. W. Blum, et al., "Findings from the National Longitudinal Study on Adolescent Health," *Journal of the American Medical Association* 278 (1997), 823–32.

2. F. I. Luntz, *What Americans Really Want . . . Really: The Truth About Our Hopes, Dreams, and Fears* (New York: Hyperion, 2009), 257.

3. Search Institute, *40 Developmental Assets for Middle Childhood (ages 8–12)* (Search Institute). www.search-institute.org/40-developmental-asset-middle-childhood-8-12.

4. Foster Cline and Jim Fay, *Parenting Teens with Love & Logic: Preparing Adolescents for Responsible Adulthood* (Colorado Springs, CO: NavPress, 2006), 14.

5. S. C. Martino, M. N. Elliott, R. Corona, D. E. Kanouse, and M. A. Schuster, "Beyond the 'Big Talk': The Roles of Breadth and Repetition in Parent-Adolescent Communication About Sexual Topics," *Pediatrics* 121 (2008), e612–e618.

6. C. M. Markham, D. Lormand, K. M. Gloppen, M. F. Peskin, B. Flores, B. Low, and L. D. House, "Connectedness as a Predictor of Sexual and Reproductive Health Outcomes for Youth," *Journal of Adolescent Health* 46 (2010), S23–S41.

7. Adapted from Gary Chapman, PhD, and Ross Campbell, MD, *The 5 Love Languages of Children*, rev. ed. (Chicago: Northfield Publishing, 2012).

8. Cline and Fay, 57.

9. L. M. Youngblade, C. Theokas, J. Schulenberg, L. Curry, I. C. Huang, and M. Novak, "Risk and Promotive Factors in Families, Schools, and Communities: A Contextual Model of Positive Youth Development in Adolescence," *Pediatrics* 119 (2007), S47–S53.

10. Resnick, et al.

11. T. S. Scheffler and P. J. Naus, "The Relationship Between Fatherly Affirmation

and a Woman's Self-Esteem, Fear of Intimacy, Comfort with Womanhood, and Comfort with Sexuality," *Canadian Journal of Human Sexuality* 8 (1999), 39–45.

12. Cline and Fay, 116.

13. M. D. Regnerus and L. B. Luchies, "The Parent-Child Relationship and Opportunities for Adolescents' First Sex," *Journal of Family Issues* 27 (2006), 159–83.

14. James Dobson, *Bringing Up Girls: Practical Advice and Encouragement for Those Shaping the Next Generation of Women* (Carol Stream, IL: Tyndale House Publishers, 2010), 95.

15. K. Magnuson and L. M. Berger, "Family Structure States and Transitions: Associations with Children's Wellbeing During Middle Childhood," *Journal of Marriage and Family* 71 (2009), 575–91.

16. US Census Bureau, *America's Families and Living Arrangements 2010* (Washington, DC: US Census Bureau, Housing and Household Economic Statistics Division, Fertility & Family Statistics Branch, 2010). www.census.gov/population/.

17. US Department of Health and Human Services, *The AFCARS Report: Preliminary FY 2009 Estimates as of July 2010* (17) (US Department of Health and Human Services, Administration for Children and Families, Administration on Children, Youth, and Families, Children's Bureau, 2010). www.acf.hhs.gov.

18. US Census Bureau, *Living Arrangements of Children Under 18 Years Old, 1960 to Present (Table CH-1)* (Washington, DC: US Census Bureau, Housing and Household Economic Statistics Division, Fertility & Family Statistics Branch, 2010). www.census.gov/population/.

19. Cline and Fay, 143–44.

20. Resnick, et al.

21. P. J. Dittus and J. Jaccard, "Adolescents' Perception of Maternal Disapproval of Sex: Relationship to Sexual Outcomes," *Journal of Adolescent Health* 26 (2000), 268–78.

22. P. S. Karofsky, L. Zeng, and M. R. Kosorock, "Relationship Between Adolescent-Parental Communication and Initiation of First Intercourse by Adolescents," *Journal of Adolescent Health* 28 (2000), 41–45.

23. Kaiser Family Foundation, *Virginity and the First Time: A Series of National Surveys of Teens About Sex* (Menlo Park, CA: Kaiser Family Foundation, 2003). www.kff.org.

24. D. J. Whitaker and K. S. Miller, "Parent-Adolescent Discussions About Sex and Condoms: Impact on Peer Influences of Sexual Risk Behavior," *Journal of Adolescent Research* 15 (2000), 251–73.

25. Ibid.

26. Dittus and Jaccard.

27. B. Albert, *With One Voice 2010: America's Adults and Teens Sound Off About Teen Pregnancy. A Periodic National Survey* (Washington, DC: National Campaign to Prevent Teen and Unplanned Pregnancy, 2010).

28. Kaiser Family Foundation.

29. B. Albert, *With One Voice 2007: America's Adults and Teens Sound Off About Teen Pregnancy* (Washington, DC: National Campaign to Prevent Teen and Unplanned Pregnancy, 2007).

30. B. Albert, *With One Voice (lite): A 2009 Survey of Adults and Teens on Parental Influence, Abstinence, Contraception, and the Increase in the Teen Birth Rate* (Washington, DC: National Campaign to Prevent Teen and Unplanned Pregnancy, 2009).

31. A. C. Robert and F. L. Sonenstein, "Adolescents' Reports of Communication with Their Parents About Sexually Transmitted Diseases and Birth Control: 1988, 1995, and 2002," *Journal of Adolescent Health* 46 (2010), 532–37.

32. M. K. Beckett, M. N. Elliott, S. Martino, D. E. Kanouse, R. Corona, D. J. Klein, and M. A. Schuster, "Timing of Parent and Child Communication About Sexuality Relative to Children's Sexual Behaviors," *Pediatrics* 125 (2010), 34–42.

33. Cline and Fay, 168.

34. R. E. Bulanda and W. D. Manning, "Parental Cohabitation Experiences and Adolescent Behavioral Outcomes," *Population Research Policy Review* 27 (2008), 593–618.

35. Dittus and Jaccard.

36. Jim Smolowe and Elaine Lafferty, "Sex with a Scorecard," *Time* Magazine, April 5, 1993. www.time.com.

37. S. S. Feldman and D. A. Rosenthal, eds., *Talking Sexuality: Parent–Adolescent Communication: New Directions for Child and Adolescent Development*, No. 97 (San Francisco, CA: Jossey-Bass, 2002), 25–26.

38. R. J. DiClemente, G. M. Wingood, R. Crosby, et al., "Parental Monitoring: Association with Adolescents' Risk Behaviors," *Pediatrics* 107 (2001), 1363–68.

39. D. A. Cohen, T. A. Farley, S. N. Taylor, D. H. Martin, and M. A. Schuster, "When and Where Do Youths Have Sex? The Potential Role of Adult Supervision," *Pediatrics* 110 (2002), e66.

40. J. G. Baker, S. L. Rosenthal, D. Leonhardt, L. M. Kollar, P. A. Succop, K. A. Burklow, and F. M. Biro, "Relationship Between Perceived Parental Monitoring and Young Adolescent Girls' Sexual and Substance Use Behaviors," *Journal of Pediatric and Adolescent Gynecology* 12 (1) (1999), 17–22.

41. J. Jaccard, P. J. Dittus, and V. V. Gordon, "Parent-Teen Communication About Premarital Sex: Factors Associated with the Extent of Communication," *Journal of Adolescent Research* 15 (2000), 187–208.

42. Feldman and Rosenthal, 25–29.

43. Albert, *With One Voice 2007*.

44. Albert, *With One Voice (lite)*.

45. A. Wiszewska, B. Pawlowski, and L. G. Boothroyd, "Father-Daughter Relationship as a Moderator of Sexual Imprinting: A Facialmetric Study," *Evolution and Human Behavior* 28 (2007), 248–52.

46. Vicki Courtney, *Logged On and Tuned Out: A Nontechie's Guide to Parenting a Tech-Savvy Generation* (Nashville, TN: B&H Publishing, 2007).

47. Joe S. McIlhaney and Freda M. Bush, *Hooked: New Science on How Casual Sex Is Affecting Our Children* (Chicago: Northfield Publishing, 2008), 125–26.

48. Commission on Children at Risk, *Hardwired to Connect: The New Scientific Case for Authoritative Communities* (New York: Institute for American Values, 2003), 17.

49. P. Y. Goodwin, W. D. Mosher, and A. Chandra, "Marriage and Cohabitation in the United States: A Statistical Portrait Based on Cycle 6 (2002) of the National Survey of Family Growth," National Center for Health Statistics, *Vital and Health Statics* 23 (2010), 8.

50. Norval Glenn and Elizabeth Marquardt, *Hooking Up, Hanging Out, and Hoping for Mr. Right: College Women on Mating and Dating Today* (New York: Institute of American Values, 2001). www.americanvalues.org/Hooking_Up.pdf.

51. L. J. Waite and M. Gallagher, *The Case for Marriage: Why Married People Are Happier, Healthier, and Better Off Financially* (New York: Doubleday, 2000).

52. Ibid., 67.

53. Ibid., 82–83.

54. R. T. Michael, J. H. Gagnon, E. O. Laumann, and G. Kolata, *Sex in America: A Definitive Survey* (Boston: Little, Brown and Company, 1994), 101.

55. Ibid., 102.

56. Ibid., 118.

57. Cline and Fay.

Chapter 10: What Are Girls to Do?

1. A. R. Giuliano and D. Salmon, "The Case for Gender-Neutral (Universal) Human Papillomavirus Vaccination Policy in the United States: Point," *Cancer Epidemiology, Biomarkers & Prevention* 17 (2008), 805–8.

2. D. D. Hallfors, M. W. Waller, D. Bauer, C. A. Ford, and C.T. Halpern, "Which Comes First in Adolescence—Sex and Drugs or Depression?" *American Journal of Preventive Medicine* 29 (2005), 163–70.

3. E. A. Impett and L. A. Peplau, "Sexual Compliance: Gender, Motivational, and Relationship Perspectives," *The Journal of Sex Research* 40 (2003), 87–100.

4. C. E. Kaestle, "Sexual Insistence and Disliked Sexual Activities in Young Adulthood: Differences by Gender and Relationship Characteristics," *Perspectives on Sexual and Reproductive Health* 41 (2009), 33–39.

5. Impett and Peplau.

6. A. Abbey, T. Zawacki, P. O. Buck, A. M. Clinton, and P. McAuslan, "Alcohol and Sexual Assault," *Alcohol Research and Health* 25 (2001), 43–51.

7. Laura Sessions Stepp, *Unhooked: How Young Women Pursue Sex, Delay Love, and Lose at Both* (New York: Penguin Group, 2007), 231–37.

8. W. F. Flack Jr., K. A. Daubman, M. L. Caron, et al., "Risk Factors and Consequences of Unwanted Sex Among University Students: Hooking Up, Alcohol, and Stress Response," *Journal of Interpersonal Violence* 22 (2007), 139–57.

9. P. Y. Goodwin, W. D. Mosher, and A. Chandra, "Marriage and Cohabitation in the United States: A Statistical Portrait Based on Cycle 6 (2002) of the National Survey of Family Growth," National Center for Health Statistics, *Vital and Health Statics* 23 (2010), 8.

10. J. Bachman, L. Johnston, and P. O'Malley, *Monitoring the Future: Questionnaire Responses from the Nation's High School Seniors 2008* (Ann Arbor, MI: The Institute for Social Research, The University of Michigan, 2009). http://monitoringthefuture.org.

11. Ibid.

12. C. Osborne, W. D. Manning, and P. J. Stock, "Married and Cohabiting Parents' Relationship Stability: A Focus on Race and Ethnicity," *Journal of Marriage and Family* 69 (2007), 1345–66.

13. W. D. Manning and S. Brown, "Children's Economic Well-being in Married and Cohabiting Parent Families," *Journal of Marriage and Family* 68 (2006), 345–62.

14. K. Kost, S. Singh, B. Vaughan, J. Trussell, and A. Bankole, "Estimates of Contraceptive Failure from the 2002 National Survey of Family Growth," *Contraception* 77 (2008), 10–21.

15. Stepp, 168–75.

16. K. A. Bogle, *Hooking Up: Sex, Dating, and Relationships on Campus* (New York: New York University Press, 2008), 52–53.

17. A. Lavinthal and J. Rozler, *The Hookup Handbook: A Single Girl's Guide to Living It Up* (New York: Simon Spotlight Entertainment, 2005), 9.

18. L. J. Waite and M. Gallagher, *The Case for Marriage: Why Married People Are Happier, Healthier, and Better Off Financially* (New York: Doubleday, 2000), 82–83.

19. G. K. Rhoades, S. M. Stanley, and H. J. Markman, "The Pre-Engagement Cohabitation Effect: A Replication and Extension of Previous Findings," *Journal of Family Psychology* 23 (2009), 107–11.

20. Osborne, et al.

21. Manning and Brown.

22. Bachman, et al.

23. The National Campaign to Prevent Teen and Unplanned Pregnancy, "Fact Sheet: How Is the 3 in 10 Statistic Calculated?" (Washington, DC: The National Campaign to Prevent Teen and Unplanned Pregnancy, 2008). www.thenationalcampaign.org.

Chapter 11: Bringing It All Together

1. This does *not* mean that if a child's tendency is to rebel, to be involved in risky behavior, or to be rude or dishonest, that we accept that as just who she is. These kinds of tendencies can result from immaturity or unhealthy influences, such as from peers, media, or abuse.

2. Benjamin Spock and Robert Needlman, *Dr. Spock's Baby and Child Care*, 8th ed. (New York: Pocket Books, 2004), 1–2.

About the Authors

JOE S. MCILHANEY, MD is a board-certified obstetrician/gynecologist who began practice in Austin, Texas, in 1968. His emphasis in his practice was care of infertile couples before that became a specialty for physicians caring for women. His work resulted in his practicing laparoscopy, microsurgery, gynecologic laser surgery, and in vitro fertilization from the earliest days of those technologies. Seeing the emotional pain his infertile couples experienced led him to found The Medical Institute for Sexual Health in 1992. He left clinical practice in 1995 to be involved with that organization full-time. He has been married to his wife, Marion, for fifty-one years. He has three incredible grown daughters and nine wonderful grandchildren.

FREDA MCKISSIC BUSH, MD, FACOG, has been involved in women's health for more than four decades. She began as a practicing OB-GYN in 1987 in Jackson, Mississippi, and is currently a clinical instructor in the department of OB-GYN and department of family medicine at the University of Mississippi Medical Center. She chairs the board of directors for The Medical Institute for Sexual Health and coauthored the book, *Hooked: New Science on How Casual Sex Is Affecting Our Children* (Northfield), with Joe S. McIlhaney, MD. She was a contributing writer to *Faith Matters: How African-American Faith Communities Can Help Prevent Teen Pregnancy* published by the National Campaign to Prevent Teen Pregnancy. Freda and her husband, Lee Bush, have been married for forty-two years; they have four children and seven grandchildren.

STAN GUTHRIE, MA is an author, columnist, editor, and literary agent. He blogs at stanguthrie.com. He has been married to Christine for twenty-four years; they have three children.

Acknowledgments

THIS BOOK COMES TO YOU from the Medical Institute for Sexual Health, without which this book would probably not have been written. Both of us have a long and intimate involvement with MI (as we call The Medical Institute), Dr. McIlhaney as its founder and Dr. Bush as current chairperson of the board of directors. Our partnership with MI worked to perfection in our previous book (*Hooked*) and again with the production of this book. The staff members at MI are all highly competent professionally and highly committed to its work. The commitment of MI's president and CEO, Art Coleman, to this project and his continual encouragement made our work a pleasure. Amy Campbell, our vice-president for finance who functions as chief operating officer, was a constant and vital help. Gladys Gonzalez, executive administrative assistant, made herself available in sacrificial ways to help bring this project to completion. Dr. Grace Ogbeche, research specialist, helped enormously by searching the scientific literature for cogent but sometimes obscure references and by constantly checking our accuracy.

No book can be written without the help of the publishing group, and we had the best with Northfield Publishing. From the very first discussion of the idea of this book the Northfield group has been very supportive. Madison Trammel and Barnabas Piper have been especially encouraging, and Annette LaPlaca's careful sensitivity to the written word fulfilled our intense desire to communicate to you, the reader.

About Stan Guthrie we cannot say enough. He worked endless hours with us to make this critical information readable. Together with the Medical Institute, we the authors have this important information, but it's another prospect altogether to be able to communicate that information well. Stan Guthrie has that gift, displayed so ably in this book. Working countless hours with a writer depends on a certain chemistry; we felt that chemistry with Stan. We hope you appreciate our partnership in writing as you read.

Jennifer Shuford, MD, worked closely with us for the year it took to write the book. She is an unusually talented and intelligent physician, with boards in both infectious disease and internal medicine, having trained at both Southwestern Medical School (Dallas) and Mayo Clinic (Rochester, MN). She holds a master's from Harvard's School of Public Health. As director of applied science at the Medical Institute from 2008 to 2010, she was a full partner with us in the production of this book in every respect, contributing research, writing, editing, and ideas. She provided outstanding first drafts of chapters three, four, five, seven, eight, and ten, as well as half of chapter one. Her intelligence, persistence, resourcefulness, and high standards strengthened the work enormously. She was an ideal collaborator and essential to the entire project.